Thank you so much for joining in our celebration!

Please accept this gift as a token of our esteem
for Bill Berman and a tangible expression of
our commitment to an ongoing Jewish conversation
about strengthening Jewish commitment
and Jewish community.

Sunday, June 3, 2007

JESNA

JEWS AND JUDAISM IN THE 21ST CENTURY

OTHER JEWISH LIGHTS BOOKS
BY EDWARD FEINSTEIN

Tough Questions Jewish Ask
A Young Adult's Guide to Building a Jewish Life

JEWS AND JUDAISM IN THE 21ST CENTURY

Human Responsibility, the Presence of God and the Future of the Covenant

Edited by Rabbi Edward Feinstein

Foreword by Paula E. Hyman

JEWISH LIGHTS Publishing

Woodstock, Vermont

Jews and Judaism in the 21st Century:
Human Responsibility, the Presence of God and the Future of the Covenant

2007 First Printing
© 2007 Valley Beth Shalom, a California nonprofit corporation

For information regarding permission to reprint material from this book, please write or fax your request to Jewish Lights Publishing, Permissions Department, at the address / fax number listed below, or e-mail your request to permissions@jewishlights.com.

Library of Congress Cataloging-in-Publication Data
Jews and Judaism in the 21st century : human responsibility, the presence of God, and the future of the covenant / edited by Edward Feinstein ; foreword by Paula Hyman.
    p. cm.
Includes bibliographical references.
  ISBN-13: 978-1-58023-315-6 (hardcover)
  ISBN-10: 1-58023-315-5 (hardcover)
1. Judaism—21st century. 2. Jews—Civilization. 3. Jews—Identity. 4. God (Judaism) 5. Covenants—Religious aspects—Judaism. I. Feinstein, Edward, 1954–

BM42.J54 2007
296.3'1172—dc22

2006103555

10 9 8 7 6 5 4 3 2 1
Manufactured in the United States of America
✿ Printed on recycled paper

Jacket Design: Jenny Buono

Published by Jewish Lights Publishing
A Division of LongHill Partners, Inc.
Sunset Farm Offices, Route 4, P.O. Box 237
Woodstock, VT 05091
Tel: (802) 457-4000   Fax: (802) 457-4004
www.jewishlights.com

CONTENTS

FOREWORD

PAULA E. HYMAN

This book invites you to eavesdrop on, and participate in, an important conversation on what makes Judaism meaningful as it faces the challenges of the twenty-first century. It brings together five prominent and dynamic rabbi-scholars of various backgrounds and perspectives to reflect on their personal, and our communal, experience of change within Judaism in our lifetime. (It is unfortunate that, while most of the contributors acknowledge the significance of the transformation in the position of women in Jewish religious and communal life, no woman's voice is heard.) The rabbis' personal stories are diverse and point to the importance of individual experience and the influence of particular teachers in how one interprets the Jewish condition. Their theologies are equally diverse, but all are willing to engage in serious conversation with each other.

In fact, what impressed me as a modern Jewish historian reading this book is the centrality of pluralism to each rabbi as he thinks about the Jewish community and about the place of Jews and Judaism in a multireligious and multiethnic world. The modern Orthodox, Conservative, Reform, and Reconstructionist rabbis speaking in this volume respect each other and affirm the authenticity of their contrasting approaches to Jewish tradition. They also make clear that pluralism does not mean relativism, that Judaism entails acceptance of some measure of obligation. This bodes well for American Jewry, although the failure of many American Orthodox leaders and the official rabbinate in Israel to approach non-Orthodox Jews as other than sinners is testimony to a fracture in world Jewry that is likely to grow. It is, unfortunately, hard to imagine many Orthodox rabbis who would seek a voice in the conversation that takes place in this book.

The recognition of religious pluralism in a globalized world has led these five Jewish spiritual leaders to affirm that religious truth is not limited to Jews and Judaism. They recognize that interfaith alliances to achieve social justice are both necessary and morally good. Interestingly, for some of the rabbis, the encounter with the stories of righteous gentiles, those non-Jews who risked their lives to save Jews during the Holocaust, has reinforced their openness to interfaith activity and understanding. Throughout Jewish history, rabbis have traditionally affirmed that Judaism was not the exclusive path to salvation. However, the historical (and well-founded) mistrust of gentiles, when combined with ignorance of their faith and resentment of their power, led Jews in many periods to disparage non-Jews as well as their religions. The recognition of the worth and merit of those whose faith differs from ours reflects not only the integration of Jews in American society but also our sense of relative security. (Even though he lives in Jerusalem, David Hartman's youth, education, and early career in America, as well as his contacts with American Jewry, are certainly important factors in his endorsement of pluralism).

The five rabbis who share their stories and philosophy with us are spokesmen for more than pluralism. Each in his own way endorses Jewish particularism, in addition to Judaism's universalism, and offers a rationale for the survival of Jews and Judaism that affirms a distinct Jewish message. This, too, reflects Jewish self-confidence. They articulate that message with different terminology, but all agree that Jews have an obligation to repair the world. In Rabbi Schulweis's formulation, "We gave the world conscience.... We gave the world a sacred humanitarianism.... We gave civilization whistle blowers against the exploitation and corruption of power." Although they differ in their definition of God, for many of the rabbis, Judaism entails a partnership with God. God needs human beings. For all of them, tending to God's creation, whether human or the planet itself, is a sacred task. And God empowers humans to take on that task, to assume responsibility for the world, as well as to withstand the misfortunes that are part of our existence.

This book is a true gift to its readers. Rabbis Ellenson, Greenberg, Hartman, Kushner, and Schulweis, as well as Rabbi Feinstein, the symposium's moderator and the book's editor, raise questions that concern thinking Jews and interpret the contemporary Jewish condition with historical, philosophical, and spiritual insight. They offer ways to understand God in human experience that will encourage further discussion. And they never talk down to us, the silent participants in the conversation.

ACKNOWLEDGMENTS

God known
not alone
but in relationship.
Not revealed through lonely power
but through our kinship, friendship
healing, binding, raising up of each other.

Rabbi Harold M. Schulweis

Our gratitude for those who made possible this great rabbinic conversation:

Founders, Harold M. Schulweis Institute
Drs. Sherri Brown *(z"l)* and David Braun
Lori and Ron Freson
Lois and Richard Gunther
Ellie and Mark Lainer
Phyllis and Ken Lemberger
Allyn and Jeff Levine
Peachy and Mark Levy
Janice Kaminar Reznik and Ben Reznik
Rita and Jack Sinder
Gail and Irv Weintraub

Symposium Sponsors

Phyllis and Sanford Beim

Sue and Rick Bender

Barbara and Dr. Richard Braun

Jacqueline and Arthur Burdorf

Nancy Sher Cohen and Robert Cohen

Beverly and Herb Gelfand

Elaine and David Gill

Paul and Sally W. Golub

Sandy and Bill Goodglick

Jewish Federation/Valley Alliance

Jewish Community Foundation

Lisa and Victor Kohn

Linda and Dr. Harvey Kulber

Irene and Howard Levine

Tammy and Jay Levine

Peachy and Mark Levy

Adele and Herb Reznikoff

Ellen and Richard Sandler

Raymond Sandler

Carol and Harvey Schulweis

Sylvia Bernstein Tregub and Burt Tregub

Mickey and Judge Joseph A. Wapner

Wells Fargo Bank, Encino

Ruth and Stan Zicklin

We thank Alys Yablon Wylen for heroic efforts editing this text. We are deeply grateful to Emily Wichland of Jewish Lights for her endless patience and commitment to this project. And to Stuart M. Matlins, publisher of Jewish Lights, for bringing this and so many works of wisdom and spirit to life, our blessings and gratitude.

THE HAROLD M. SCHULWEIS INSTITUTE

Library
Scholars Series
Global Outreach
Cultural Arts

The Harold M. Schulweis Institute
A Center for Jewish Learning

The Harold M. Schulweis Institute—A Center for Jewish Learning, at Valley Beth Shalom in Encino, California, was created to share with generations to come Rabbi Harold M. Schulweis's vision of Jewish life and Jewish learning. The Institute maintains actual and online (www.hmsi.info) libraries to collect, preserve, and disseminate Rabbi Schulweis's writings and oratory; offers scholar programs, public dialogues, and participation in global social issues; and promotes enrichment of Jewish and synagogue life through visual and performing arts, music, and literature.

PART I

HOW HAVE YOU CHANGED? HOW HAVE WE CHANGED?

When the Chasidic master, Reb Yaakov Yitzchak, the "Seer of Lublin," died, his disciples divided his worldly goods. One got his books, one his Kiddush *cup, another his* tallis. *There remained one humble Chasid. To him was given the rebbe's clock.*

On his way home, the Chasid stopped at an inn. When he discovered he had no money to pay the innkeeper, he offered the rebbe's clock as payment. The innkeeper installed the clock in one of the rooms.

A year later, another of the rebbe's Chasidim passed by and stayed at the inn. All night, he could not sleep. All night, the innkeeper heard the restless footsteps of the Chasid pacing the floor.

In the morning, the worried innkeeper inquired of his guest, "Was there something wrong with the room?" The

1

Chasid replied anxiously, "The clock, where did you get the clock?" The innkeeper related the story.

"I knew it!" responded the Chasid. "This clock belonged to the Seer. It is a holy clock. All other clocks in the world mark time from the past—they measure us from where we've come. This clock ticks toward the future. Every time I lay down to rest, the clock reminded me how much more there is to do before redemption can be realized."

It's all in how we read the clock. Judaism has always pointed toward the past—preserving, conserving, protecting the past. The Jewish people have been committed, perhaps obsessed, with the task of carrying the values and wisdom of the past into the future.

The generation of the late twentieth century has experienced a rupture in Jewish time. Our confrontation with modernity, the integration of Jews into the American mainstream, the shattering tragedy of the Holocaust, and the rebirth of a Jewish state in the Land of Israel were all experienced by this one generation. Suddenly, the Jewish clock doesn't work. We can no longer look easily to our past, as have the generations before us, for lessons of faith, models of Jewish meaning, and an understanding of the collective Jewish project. Nor can we confidently project ourselves into the future. So much of what was taken for granted in earlier times is now open to question.

The five thinkers represented in this volume, Rabbi David Ellenson, Rabbi Irving "Yitz" Greenberg, Rabbi David Hartman, Rabbi Harold Kushner, and Rabbi Harold Schulweis, are all witnesses to the cataclysmic history of twentieth-century Jewry. As communal leaders and rabbinic teachers, they have experienced the breach in Jewish time and meaning. In response, each has attempted to repair, rewind, and reset the Jewish clock. In March 2005, they gathered at Valley Beth Shalom in Encino, California, on the occasion of the celebration of Harold M. Schulweis's eightieth birthday. They were each asked to address two questions: How have you changed? How have we changed? The best of these four days of lectures and dialogues are gathered here. The significance of what was said at this celebration was much greater than the event itself. Five prominent rabbis grappled with the deepest issues that face the Jewish people as we face the new century.

The five thinkers whose work composes this collection represent a broad spectrum of contemporary Jewish experience. Rabbis Schulweis and Kushner were educated at The Jewish Theological Seminary of America, intellectual heart of the Conservative Movement. Both were students and disciples of Mordecai M. Kaplan, and both have enjoyed outstanding careers as pulpit rabbis. Rabbis Greenberg and Hartman were raised in the Orthodox community and were educated at Yeshiva University, where they studied with the "Rav," Joseph B. Soloveitchik. Following a career as a pulpit rabbi, Rabbi Hartman made *aliyah* to Israel in 1970, where he taught at the Hebrew University and founded the Shalom Hartman Institute. Rabbi Greenberg pursued a unique career path as the founder of CLAL—the National Jewish Center for Learning and Leadership and as mentor to the Jewish Federation organizations of North America. Rabbi Ellenson, raised in an Orthodox community, received his rabbinic ordination at the Reform Movement's Hebrew Union College–Jewish Institute of Religion, where he taught Jewish thought, until assuming that institution's presidency.

Coming from such diverse backgrounds and experiences, these five rabbis arrive at a consensus in their responses to the dilemma of contemporary Jewry. To address the "eclipse of God" of the late twentieth century, each reaffirms the centrality of human responsibility in Jewish spiritual life. Human moral action is our revelation of God's presence in the world. The tragedy of the Holocaust and the ecstasy of the rebirth of Israel have led each of them to envision a new stage in the development of the ancient covenant, a stage in which human beings take responsibility for shaping the Jewish historical experience as God's partners in the work of *tikkun* (healing). How this new sense of the centrality of human responsibility finds expression in the rhythms of Jewish personal and communal life—its implications for halachah, for prayer, for the synagogue and for the denominations of Jewish life, for life in the State of Israel, as well as for our relations with the non-Jewish world—animates these fascinating conversations.

Two millennia ago, amid the smoke and rubble of the destroyed Temple, a group of scholars gathered to rethink the collective Jewish project and its meaning. That great conversation, the essence of the Talmud, reset the Jewish clock and renewed a Jewish future. Now once again, a group of gifted scholars gather to reinterpret the Jewish project, to reassert its meaning, reenvision its institutions, and reimagine its future. A circle of rabbis gather to reset the Jewish clock. The Jewish clock is an alarm clock, set to awaken us to a new sense of responsibility and to the possibilities of a new day.

RABBI HAROLD M. SCHULWEIS

Harold M. Schulweis is widely regarded as among the most successful and influential synagogue leaders in his generation. Early in his career, Rabbi Schulweis recognized that the contemporary synagogue held the power to mediate meaning to a generation of Jews isolated from community and alienated from tradition by the rhythms of American life and the spiritually corrosive elements of American culture. Beginning in 1970, Rabbi Schulweis used his pulpit at Valley Beth Shalom in suburban Los Angeles as a laboratory to introduce a series of synagogue innovations that spread widely among American congregations. These include synagogue-based *chavurot*—small groupings of families sharing intimacy, learning, and celebration; "para-rabbinics"—a revolutionary model of lay-professional cooperation; "Response"—a support structure welcoming gays and lesbians and their families into the synagogue; *"Keruv"*—a vigorous outreach to unaffiliated Jews and "unchurched" Christians.

Born in the Bronx, New York, in 1925 and educated at Yeshiva College, The Jewish Theological Seminary of America, New York University, and the Pacific School of Religion in Berkeley, California, Rabbi Schulweis taught philosophy at

City College of New York before taking pulpits in Parkchester, New York; Oakland, California; and Encino, California. He provides a rare example of a consummate "public intellectual" within the Jewish community.

In his theological writing, Rabbi Schulweis advocates a conception of "theological humanism." Based on the biblical conviction that the human being bears the divine image, and Buber's concept of God revealed in deep human relationships, Rabbi Schulweis locates God not above but within and between human beings. The focus of religious experience and reflection, for Rabbi Schulweis, is not a personal God but Godliness. Conscience is the most powerful expression of Covenant.

In the late 1960s, Rabbi Schulweis was introduced to a Jewish family rescued and hidden from the Nazis by German Christians. Upon inquiry, he discovered that the rescuers were never recognized or appreciated by the Jewish community. He founded the Jewish Foundation for the Righteous to celebrate the heroic goodness of Christians who rescued Jews in Nazi-occupied Europe. The foundation has located and acknowledged thousands of Christian rescuers.

In 2005, Rabbi Schulweis founded the Jewish World Watch, gathering more than fifty congregations of all denominations to respond to genocide in Sudan. Jewish World Watch is dedicated to cultivating the conscience of the Jewish and world community in the face of the twenty-first century's first genocide.

GLOBALISM AND THE JEWISH CONSCIENCE

RABBI HAROLD M. SCHULWEIS

In response to the question "How have I changed? How have we changed?" I would like to address the notion of globalism and Judaism. As the *Zohar* instructed: "There is nothing in the world empty of God." With that in mind we must pay careful attention to current events, and realize that all events have meaning, and they all have something to teach us.

When the Industrial Revolution took place, for example, it overwhelmed the world of the shtetl, the Jewish village. It is told that the disciples in one shtetl asked the rabbi, "What can we learn from the invention of the train, the telegraph, and the telephone?" The rabbi answered, "From the train, we learn that, but for one moment, everything can be lost. Once the door of the train is closed, you miss the great journey. Pay attention!"

They asked, "And what can you learn from the telegraph?" and the rabbi answered, "From the telegraph you learn that every word counts. Guard your tongue!"

"And what can you learn from the telephone?"

"From the telephone you learn that whatever you speak here is heard there. Words have consequences."

We live in the age of globalization—economic, political, cultural, and technological globalization. What meaning does globalization have for us? It has entered our life, the life of our country, the life of world civilizations. This is the age of the Internet, satellite television, computers, cell phones, e-mail, and outsourcing. The world is smaller and more interconnected than ever before in its history. Things move faster. Space is more constricted. Geography has shrunk. What happens in Baghdad affects California. What happens in Darfur affects Washington. What happens in Indonesia affects Iowa.

What does globalization mean? Historian Francis Fukuyama, in his book *End of History*, argues that globalism means that economics, in the future and in the present, is more powerful than politics. The Soviet Union imploded, not because a single missile was shot, but because it could not bear the burden of its command economy. Trade unity will do what politics did not do before globalization.

On the other hand, Professor Samuel Huntington, in *The Clash of Civilizations*, writes that globalism not only stabilizes, but also destabilizes the world. Jihad and McWorld occur at the same time and are linked together, driven by technology, ecology, communication, and congress. Huntington foresees not global harmony, but tribal factionalism, the clash of civilizations. The world is falling apart—the center will not hold.

What about us? Judaism is a religion of meaning. What does Judaism have to say about the phenomenon of globalization?

Judaism speaks to the entire world because it is a global religion. Consider the different calendars of various religions. For Christianity, this is 2006 *anno Domini* (in the year of our Lord). It marks the birth of Jesus as the Son of God. Muslims begin their calendar differently, with 622 AD, which dates back to Muhammad's Hajira, his flight from Mecca to

8

Medina. But the Jewish calendar celebrates not the birth of a Jewish savior, not the birth of a Jewish redeemer, not even a Jewish event such as the Exodus out of Egypt or the revelation of the Law at Sinai. Rather, Rosh Hashanah, the Jewish New Year, celebrates the birth of the universe and humanity.

The first eleven chapters of the book of Genesis deal not with a Jew—not with Abraham or Isaac or Jacob or Moses or Aaron—but with Adam, the archetype of humanity. Adam is not a Jew; his name is derived from *adamah*, which means "earth." The Sages ask, "From which place in the universe was this earth taken? Was it from Athens or Rome or Jericho?" The answer is that it was taken from four corners of the earth: north, south, east, and west. And what was the color of this clay that formed the human being? Our sages answered, "It was black, and white, and red, and yellow."

God did not create religion. God created the universe and, within the universe, humanity. And the singular biblical verse that resonates throughout Judaism and world history is Genesis 1:27: "God created every human being [man, woman, child] in God's image." Whatever color, whatever race, whatever ethnicity. God created every human being with divine potentiality.

There were other traditions that believed that some people were informed by God. The Egyptian pharaoh believed that he himself was God. The kings of Sumeria believed that they were gods. But in Judaism, every single human being is created by God—prince and pauper, mighty and weak. Adam is not created as different species or kinds. Adam is one. There is only one humanity and only one universe and only one God and only one universal obligation.

In the Midrash it is written: "When the Holy Blessed One created the world, God took Adam around to see the trees of the Garden of Eden, which included the Tree of Life and the

Tree of Knowledge, and God said to Adam, *'Behold My work. All this I create for you. Take care you do not destroy it, for if you do, there is no one left to repair it.'"* This charge is addressed to every man, to every human being, so that every human being can say, "For my sake was the world created." For when the Rabbis asked, "Why did God create Adam singly, by himself, and not as part of a family?" the Rabbis answered, "So that no one should say, 'My ancestor is superior to yours.'"

Textbooks treat Christianity and Islam as universal religions, but not Judaism. From Spinoza to Kant to Hegel, and to many Jews and non-Jews, Judaism is considered ethnic, small and provincial, tribal—concerned only with its own believers and well-being and with no one else.

We are a small people with a big idea. When Egypt, by 3000 BCE, had built its pyramids, and Sumer had its huge empires, we Jews were a tiny band of nomads milling around the upper regions of the Arabian Desert. When this small people finally settled down in the Promised Land, it was 150 miles in length, from Dan to Beersheva, and 50 miles across. But significantly, this small people accepted God's majestic agenda.

If you believe in a global God, you must pay attention to the entire world and humanity: God's world is populated by 6 billion people. One-sixth of the world's people, 22 percent, live below the poverty line; 1.3 billion human beings have no access to safe drinking water; 2.6 billion live without elementary sanitation; 841 million people are severely malnourished; 150 million people go to bed hungry every night; 30,000 children will die today, as they will every day, from starvation, from lack of shelter, from poverty. You can't close the newspaper once you believe in a global God. For if you close the newspaper, you make God's world irrelevant. If you close the newspaper, you make a mockery out of prayer and repentance and goodness. A synagogue of prayer must have a window, not a mirror. A window to look out at the world.

If I close the window of the newspaper, I close the character of Jewish world religion. What shall I say to my children and my grandchildren, who will ask after Rwanda and Darfur, "Where was the synagogue? The rabbis? The congregations?" What shall we say to ourselves, we who rightfully asked, "Where were the priests, the pastors, the Pope?"

Our greatness as a religion is that we Jews conceived of ourselves as God's allies, partners, and friends. We gave the world conscience. We gave to the world a sacred universalism that remains at the foundation of our relationship with the world. Our prophets cared about the ethical behavior of the Ammonites, Hittites, Syrians, and Babylonians. Our last prophet, Malachi, spoke to the world population: "Have we not one Father? Did not one God create us all?" (Malachi 2:10). "Did not God who made me in my mother's belly make him? Did not one God form us both in the womb?" (Job 31:15).

How else can I understand our tradition, which on the very first day of Rosh Hashanah speaks of Hagar and Ishmael, not as Jews, but as a mother and a son who are protected by the angel of the Universal God? How else can we explain that our Sages chose for us to read the book of Jonah, which chastises the Jewish prophet Jonah for his unwillingness to preach to the citizens of Nineveh, who are the enemies of God? How else can I explain the grandeur of Abraham's challenge to God in defense no less of pagans, those of Sodom and Gomorrah?

Judaism gave the world not ziggurats or pyramids or mausoleums, but compassion and responsibility. We gave the world a sacred humanitarianism. We gave the world an economy that commands us to set aside a corner of a field, a corner of the harvest, for the poor, to see to it that the forgotten seed not be scrounged up from the fields, but let to lie for the hungry. We gave the world the notion of tithing. We gave to the world dignity, empathy, and economic justice. In Exodus, we read: "And if you take from your neighbor a cloak as a pledge, you must return it to him at sunset, because his cloak is the only covering that he has" (Exodus 22:25–26).

We gave civilization whistle-blowers against the exploitation and corruption of power. The Jewish prophet Amos cried out against tyranny: "For they ripped open the pregnant woman.... They sell the righteous for silver, and the needy for a pair of shoes. They trample the head of the poor into the dust of the earth and turn aside the way of the afflicted" (Amos 1:13, 2:6–7).

We gave the world unique heroes who were not philosophers searching for a definition or miracle men promising life after death, but people who emphasized the goal of all life here and now. The prophet touched the ethical nerve and chastised the kings of all nations, including Judah, to protest the lot of the poor, the widow, the orphan, the sick here in God's world. The Jewish religious hero adopted God's agenda as his own—and it became our agenda.

In the late 1960s, I was invited by the West German government to visit Germany and see its progress after the conclusion of the Second World War. In Berlin I met with German theological students—young men who urged me (for what reason I knew not) to visit with D. Otto Dibellius, the bishop of Berlin Brandenburg. I came to his large home, and because I had just visited the Dachau concentration camp, I turned to him and said, "Bishop, what did you do on Kristallnacht when the synagogues and temples and houses were destroyed by the Nazis? What did you do when so many Jews were placed in jail?"

The bishop looked at me and said, "You are a rabbi, and you should know that it is my first obligation to protect the well-being of my church." I asked him about the crucifixion, about sacrifice for fellow human beings, about Christian compassion, and he answered, "As a bishop, my primary concern was with my church and its people." I came home from Germany having learned a most valuable lesson: beware of spiritual narcissism, and overcome religious selfishness and religious tribalism.

Sifting through the ashes of the Shoah, searching for an ember of hope, I came across Philip Friedman's *Their Brothers' Keepers*. This pioneer work opened a new world for me. There were tears here, but from out of a different well. Here were peasants, priests, farmers, and teachers who *refused* to rationalize complicity with the predators. Here were Christians from all walks of life and in every Nazi-controlled country who forged passports, hid Jewish families, fed the hungry, the hunted. Who were they? What kind of Poles, Germans, Dutch, Belgians, Bulgarians, Christians would risk their lives and their families to save a people not of their own faith, and of a tradition often deemed antagonistic to their church tradition?

Throughout the 1960s I found myself increasingly drawn to the phenomenon of the rescue of Jews by non-Jews. I spoke to rabbinic and lay audiences and appealed to national Jewish organizations and secular academic circles to engage in a serious empirical study and moral interpretation of these acts of altruism in the midst of the unspeakable atrocities of the Holocaust. It led me to found and chair the Institute for Righteous Acts, some of whose archives are housed at the Judah Magnes Museum in Berkeley.

For some, the challenge of confronting gentile goodness may be further complicated because the heroes are not Jews.

That mindset reveals "split thinking." The lure to divide the world into two parts, the Manichean temptation to divide the world into children of darkness and children of light, is seductive. The schismatic thinking that "blackwashes" outsiders and "whitewashes" insiders simplifies our disappointments and anger. Confronted by righteous gentiles, we face a mottled reality. The outside is not entirely darkness and treachery. The rescuers upset the split mentality that revels in the syntax of "all or none," "always or never." The denial and avoidance of gentile altruism perseveres at perilous cost.

But six decades after the Holocaust, some people are now emboldened to enter the cavern with a small lantern, sift through the ashes of crematoria, and find some residue of hope. Slowly, a literature of scholarly research and popular acknowledgment of the acts of the righteous is emerging. Nechama Tec has published a pioneer study on Christian rescue of Jews in Nazi-occupied Poland, *When Light Pierced the Darkness*. Douglas K. Huneke's book *The Moses of Rovno* tells the stirring story of Hermann Graebe, a German Christian who risked his own life and the lives of his family to lead hundreds of Jews to safety during the Holocaust. Professor Samuel Oliner has authored a wide-ranging research on the altruistic personality, based on in-depth interviews of gentile rescuers. Pierre Sauvage's documentary of André Trocmé and the rescuers in the French village of Le Chambon and Spielberg's film *Schindler's List* are widely celebrated. There are hopeful signs that the passive resistance and converging biases against research and publicity of the righteous gentile may be changing.

On moral grounds alone, neglect of the altruistic phenomenon must be overcome. Jews, witnesses to the capabilities of human beings to torture and destroy, are also witnesses to the human capacities to save and rebuild. That double witness is vital for healing the traumatized conscience of humanity. The post-Holocaust generation, the children of those who survived, needs help to trust again. The precarious imbalance that places all weight of evidence on the depressive side of the scale may be corrected by the empirical evidence of human benevolence. The prejudice that distorts the character of human nature and confines it to the "nasty, brutish, and short" must be countered by the testimony of those who in hellish times experienced long-term, self-sacrificing care and concern.

Research on altruistic behavior must be supported; greater attention must be paid to this repeatedly neglected area of Holocaust studies. The evidence of rescue does not trivialize the monstrosity of evil. There are no heroes without villains, no rescue of the hunted without pursuit by the hunters. To the contrary, those Jews and non-Jews who may fear entering the cave lest they be enveloped by the despair of no exit may be encouraged to overcome their crippling fear. Light is needed to illumine the darkness. Moral heroes of flesh and blood are needed to resuscitate our exhausted morale.

An ironic symmetry yet surrounds us. The denial or denigration of the numbers of righteous gentiles who helped is the reverse side of the pernicious denial and minimizing of the numbers of victims who suffered. One cries that there were not so many victims; the other cries that there were not so many heroes. There are always too few moral heroes, always too few of the righteous whose presence could have saved Sodom. That makes the memory of those few all the more precious, all the more important. The memory of the righteous must not be swept away with the wicked, surely not by heirs to a tradition that declares that for the sake of thirty-six righteous people the world is preserved. The thirty-six among us must be honored.

Our post-Holocaust task is to retrieve the meaning of the acts of the rescuers of our generation, to discover their fate and sweeten the remainder of their lives. The rescuers who transcended their environment are too significant to our civilization to be unsung and uncared for.

The study and teaching of altruism in our times are sacred theological moments not to be lost in the debris of the Holocaust. Those memories give soul to the body of historical facts. As the historian Yosef Yerushalmi observes in his book *Zakhor: Jewish History and Jewish Memory,* "The choice for Jews as for non-Jews is not whether or not to have a past but what kind of past shall one have" ([Seattle: University of Washington Press, 1982], p. 99). While history is irreversible, we have the power to decide what of our past belongs in our future. To choose a past is not to dissemble, but to release the future from the grip of the past. *Hakarat hatov,* "the recognition of goodness," the revelations of the unrecorded altruistic acts of anonymous men and women, is important not only for historical integrity, but for the meaning and morals of our lives. The history of the Holocaust calls us to keep faithfully "a double memory ... a memory of the best and of the worst" (Camus). Repression of either side of the ledger distorts history and paralyzes the future. Ours is the mandate of *hakarat hatov,* the recognition of goodness in a world where goodness is interred with the anonymous bones in the grave of history. We single out those Christian rescuers of our people who, during the hellish nightmare of the Holocaust, risked life and limb— their own, and that of their families—to protect a people not of their fate or faith. Therefore, we must search out these Christian moral heroes, raise attention to their courageous narratives, and see to it that in their waning years they receive the gratitude of our people and stipends to prolong their lives with dignity. We honor heroes from the "other side."

Today in Darfur, in the Sudan, we are witness to the first genocide of the twenty-first century. People are being killed, raped, and tortured every day. A million people have already been forcibly displaced—two hundred thousand refugees with nowhere to go. Men, women, and children die of starvation— thirty thousand dead in only eighteen months. The *janjaweed* militia of Sudan continues to destroy, pillage, torture. *Janjaweed* is an Arabic term that is translated "a devil on horseback with a gun," which brings to mind the Cossacks and the pogroms of Chmielnicki.

We took an oath, "Never again!" Was this vow to protect only Jews from the curse of genocide? God forbid that our children and grandchildren ask of us, "Where was the synagogue during Rwanda, when genocide took place and eight hundred thousand people were slaughtered in one hundred days?"

Can we throw out the newspapers? Do we dare shut our eyes and ears so as not to see or hear what is going on in God's world? After the Shoah, we know. The real question is not, "Why doesn't God intervene?" The question is, "Why do God's partners, into whose nostrils God breathed divine potentiality, pretend that they are mute, paralyzed, deaf, impotent?"

"Few are guilty," my teacher Rabbi Abraham Joshua Heschel wrote, "but all are responsible." We are responsible to protect each other, to love and protect the stranger, the pariah, the weak, those of another color, those of another faith. We need to cry out to the world and to influence the world, beginning with ourselves, to mandate them, "Lay not your hands upon the innocent. Do not do anything to harm them, for they are God's children."

At stake is humanity. At stake is the universe. At stake is the stature of God. How big is our God? The Rabbis interpreted the verse *Adonai tzilchah*, "God is your shadow,"

(Psalm 121:5) to mean the following: If you stand bent down, then the shadow of God will be contracted and shriveled, but if you stand erect, the shadow will expand, grow mighty and enlarged." As we stand, God will be elevated. We live in God's shadow and God's shadow lives in us.

We Jews who hear with ancient ears know that silence is lethal. We must know in order to do. And we must do in order to change the world. We know how essential raising our voice is. We know that silence is lethal and feigned laryngitis, wicked.

We knew what we wanted the church to do. We wanted them to protest, to fast, to stand before embassies, and to chain their hands to iron fences. Can we do less? We can protest. We can use our voice to pierce the callousness of society. We can take our fasts from Yom Kippur into the streets and into the marketplace. As the liturgy says, "Is this the fast that I have given you, but to break every yolk, to deal bread to starving infants, to break down the curtains of indifference?"

We must urge goodness to be enacted in our own lives, in the first genocide of the twenty-first century, in Darfur. How can its anguish not remind us of our sacred oath, "Never again"? How can we, who witnessed the conspiracy of silence, bite our tongue and feign muteness?

The two issues discussed here—acknowledging Righteous Christians, the heroes of the twentieth century's Holocaust, and responding to the first genocide of the twenty-first—share many values, but especially their common roots in the soil of Jewish conscience. I believe the character of Jewish conscience is unparalleled in world religions. In biblical and rabbinic language, what we call "conscience" is translated as *yirat Elohim*, "the awe of Godliness." That awe is the unique subterranean wellspring in Jewish moral theology. The distinctive quality of spiritual audacity in the Jewish tradition is of ultimate significance in a world where blind obedience to authoritarian powers, secular or religious, is held to be the major mark of piety and patriotism.

Here is a Jewish particularistic universalism:

To be a Jew is to think big.
To be a Jew is to think globally.
To be a Jew is to act globally.
To be a Jew is to love God, who is global.

Baruch atah Adonai, Eloheinu Melech ha'olam, "Blessed art Thou, *Adonai* our God, Ruler of the entire universe." Ruler of this universe. God's universe is not to be escaped, or denied, or demeaned. The universe is to be sanctified.

RABBI DAVID ELLENSON

Rabbi David Ellenson, president of Hebrew Union College–Jewish Institute of Religion (HUC-JIR) and I. H. and Anna Grancell Professor of Jewish Religious Thought, is a distinguished rabbi, scholar, and leader of the Reform Movement, internationally recognized for his publications and research in the areas of Jewish religious thought, ethics, and modern Jewish history. Rabbi Ellenson received his PhD from Columbia University in 1981 and holds MA degrees from Columbia University, HUC-JIR, and the University of Virginia. He received his BA from the College of William and Mary in Virginia in 1969.

Rabbi Ellenson is a fellow at the Shalom Hartman Institute of Jerusalem and a fellow and lecturer at the Institute of Advanced Studies at Hebrew University in Jerusalem. He has published and lectured extensively on diverse topics in modern Jewish history, ethics, and thought.

Rabbi Ellenson's work describes the writings of Reform, Conservative, Orthodox, and Reconstructionist leaders in Europe, the United States, and Israel during the nineteenth and twentieth centuries and employs a sociological approach to illuminate the history and development of modern Jewish religious denominationalism. His application of this method has allowed him to emphasize the interplay between Jewish religious tradition and modern society in unique ways and has prompted him to write and lecture on diverse topics, including early Reform and Orthodox Judaism in nineteenth-century Germany, conversion to Judaism at the beginning of the 1900s, and the problems of medical ethics in present-day America. His academic lectures have been delivered at such institutions as Charles University in Prague, Ben-Gurion and Bar-Ilan Universities in Israel, Haverford College, Harvard University, Yale University, Brown University, and The Jewish Theological Seminary of America.

Born in Brookline, Massachusetts, in 1947, Rabbi Ellenson was raised in Newport News, Virginia. He is married to Rabbi Jacqueline Koch Ellenson, who was ordained at HUC-JIR/New York in 1983. They are the parents of Ruth, Micah, Hannah, Naomi, and Raphael.

BUILDING A WORLD IN WHICH GOD WOULD BE HAPPY TO LIVE

RABBI DAVID ELLENSON

All authentic theology must come from the depths of one's own soul, and I will therefore frame my remarks in an autobiographical form. I would like to speak about my own understanding of and approach to Judaism, and I would like to share with you the people and the thinkers who have helped shape my own opinions about Judaism, our people, and the world. I believe that theology is ultimately an expression of autobiography and that how we think about God and how we think about our ultimate commitments are so bound up with our own personal story that it is disingenuous to pretend that there is somehow an objective place outside of the self that can serve as an Archimedean point for theological reflection. All of us are existentially bounded by the contexts and persons that have informed and sustained us, and by our personal responses and reactions to them.

My own approach to Judaism cannot be described or explained without recourse to the family in which I was raised. I grew up in an Orthodox synagogue in Newport News, Virginia, with parents who were passionately committed to Zionism and the State of Israel, to Jewish religious tradition and learning, and to *Klal Yisrael* and the larger human community. As a result, I have had and continue to have numerous Jewish affiliations in my life. I was ordained at the Hebrew Union College, and I am currently a member of the Reconstructionist Rabbinical Association as well as the Reform Central Conference of American Rabbis. I have lived for a year at Kibbutz Mishmar Haemek, a *Hashomer Hatzair* kibbutz (anti-religious socialist collective), and I have served as a visiting professor at both The Jewish Theological Seminary and the Hebrew University in Jerusalem. During our years in Los Angeles, my family and I belonged both to Leo Beck Temple (Reform) and Congregation Beth Am (Conservative). Our children have—at various times and in light of how we viewed their needs—attended Sinai-Akiba Academy, Emanuel Day School, Pressman Academy, the Milken Community High School, and a variety of camps and day camps under Orthodox, Conservative, Reform, and Zionist auspices. As a result, it might be easy to conclude that I actually have no principles. However, I would rather view these transitions and journeys into different sectors of the Jewish world as reflecting a commitment to Jewish pluralism and as an affirmation that there is something of value in virtually every sector of the Jewish world—that no one group has a monopoly on truth.

This last statement stems from my conviction that all religious expression that we put forth is by definition penultimate. If God is transcendent and infinite, as I believe the Holy One is, then all our human attempts to understand God and walk in the ways of the Divine are at best partial expressions of truth. Sparks of God's holiness can be found throughout creation, and our task is to search for them and gather them up in every corner where we encounter them.

These beliefs and deeds were undoubtedly shaped by my boyhood in Virginia. I grew up there in a small Southern

Jewish community. My paternal grandparents had come to the United States from Lithuania, and after entering the United States, they migrated southward to Newport News, where my grandfather, a tinsmith, opened a roofing company. My father was the youngest of five children, and he attended the College of William and Mary in Virginia. After World War II, my father attended Harvard University Law School, and there he met my mother, a native of Cambridge, Massachusetts, at a Friday-night Hillel service and dinner. My father and mother immediately fell in love and wanted to become engaged. However, according to family lore, my grandmother in Boston would not allow the engagement. She said that she had never heard of a Jew from Virginia and that she would not allow the engagement until she met his mother. My mother responded by asking my Bubbe Stern how my father could *not* be Jewish? She said, "His name is Sam, he has an eastern-European Jewish face, he speaks Yiddish, and I met him at Hillel." Nevertheless, my maternal grandmother remained steadfast in her determination not to permit the engagement, saying that none of these facts were conclusive in any way. After all, she reasoned, Harvard boys are quite smart, and he may have simply learned Yiddish and gone to Hillel for the express purpose of meeting a Jewish girl. Until she met his mother there would be no engagement.

So my Bubbe Ellenson soon made the eighteen-hour train ride from Newport News to Boston. My paternal grandmother was a stocky woman and unmistakably eastern-European Jewish. When she arrived in Boston and disembarked from the train, my parents and my maternal grandmother were there, and my father ran over to his mother and embraced her. At that moment, my Bubbe Stern took a look at this other woman and said to my mother, "Is that Sam's mother?" My mother then said, "Well, I suppose it is. They're kissing, they're hugging, and they're speaking Yiddish to one another." My grandmother from Boston then turned to my mother and said, "OK—the engagement's on." And now her grandson heads a Reform seminary that embraces patrilineal descent—fairly graphic testimony to the changes that have marked American Judaism during these past sixty years!

I was born during my father's senior year in law school. We returned to Newport News after his graduation, and there I was raised. There were four synagogues in Newport News. One was an Orthodox synagogue with a *mechitza*, a ritual barrier separating men and women during prayer. Another was an Orthodox synagogue that lacked a *mechitza*. The rabbi of that congregation was a graduate of Yeshiva University, and they used the Birnbaum Siddur. However, men and women sat together during services, an unthinkable practice in an American Orthodox synagogue today. There was also a Conservative temple. Unlike most places in the South, the very last synagogue to emerge there was a Reform temple, which was established in 1955. My family belonged to the Orthodox synagogue with the *mechitza*, and the education I received was an Orthodox one. "Torah-true" was synonymous with Judaism for me. I learned a lot from this childhood, and I remain grateful in so many ways for the education I received.

My one critique was that while it was clear that many of my teachers loved Judaism, Jews themselves did not come out as well. That is, my teachers frequently complained about the laxity in observance that marked most Jews, and the implication was that they were "evil," or surely "severely lacking" in a significant way. Years later, when I read Rabbi Irving "Yitz" Greenberg's book, *In the Image of God*, I was very, very touched by a childhood story that he told about his own father, one that stands in such sharp contrast with the ethos that marked my own teachers. Rabbi Greenberg, if I remember correctly, said that once during his own childhood in the 1940s, he had complained about the Jews of his day to his father, and with all the fervor of an adolescent, he complained about how unobservant they were. After listening to Yitz's tirade, his father observed that if Yitz was going to compare the performance of the Jews and God during the Holocaust, then perhaps the Jewish people had done better.

No wonder that, years later, a critic could say of Rabbi Greenberg that his greatest fault is "that he loves Jews too much." *Halevai* (if only!) that all Jewish leaders should be like this, for the lesson I draw from this story is that it is crucial for anyone who would be a Jewish leader to love people, and that all theology—authentic theology—must begin with people. If a religion does not instruct you to embrace others, then it has to be, by definition, of limited or no utility. As a boy, I had the most difficult time not with the beauty of the ritual to which I was introduced, but with the lack of appreciation for the wonder of both the frailty and the greatness that inform the human condition.

There was another "problematic dimension" to the Judaism I experienced as a child and that I felt keenly as I began to mature and reflect on my own Jewishness. The Judaism to which I was introduced as a boy focused almost exclusively on ritual concerns. I like rituals and I enjoy their performance very much. They play a significant role in my life and help me forge my identity as a Jew. However, for the leaders of my congregation, these ritual concerns seemed to be the "be-all and end-all" of Judaism. And here I was, a boy growing up in the South during the 1950s and 1960s, in a town at a time where "colored people" and "white people" would sit in different sections on buses and in restaurants as well as in movie theaters. There were water fountains marked "Colored

Only," and others that were labeled "White Only." These were times of great ethical turmoil, and my teachers told me on more than one occasion that as Jew I should be concerned principally with *mitzvot*, that is, *mitzvot ma'asiyot*, "ritual commandments," and that matters such as desegregation should not be of primary concern for me. All of this is of course incredibly idiosyncratic and may well reflect nothing more than my own subjective way of internalizing Judaism during those formative years of my life. However, this approach—as I understood it—embodied a tremendously constricted way of approaching Jewish tradition. Indeed, one of the things I have always most admired about Harold Schulweis is that he has used his pulpit to teach that there is a Jewish imperative to combine the particularistic and universalistic elements, the ritual and ethical dimensions, of our Jewish tradition.

After all, the notion of covenant stands as the very foundational idea of Jewish religious tradition. This notion emphasizes that there is a partnership that exists between God and all humanity on the one hand, and between God and the Jewish people on the other—there is the sense that Jews and gentiles are *shutafim* (partners) with the Divine in the work of creation.

One of the most audacious and meaningful teachings in Judaism is that God stands in covenantal relationship with all human beings—not just Jews. There is the idea of what the Rabbis call the Noahide Covenant, which is taken as a sign that a covenant indeed exists between God and all persons. There could hardly be a greater religious expression of the universal ideal that is so crucial to Jewish tradition.

At the same time, we have mention in Genesis 15 of the *b'rit bein hab'tarim*—the covenant between the pieces—that marks the particular relationship between Abraham and his descendants and God. Rabbi Schulweis teaches us that an authentic Judaism needs to appreciate both these poles—the universal and the particular. Jewish identity and community dissolve in a Judaism that is focused exclusively on universal concerns. Such a Judaism fails to appreciate that persons are embedded in particular ways in the world. At the same time, we are required to look beyond the particularity of our own community and extend our concerns to the larger world. Rabbi Schulweis himself embodies this very balance between the particular and the universal, and I often wonder if, as a boy, I had had a rabbi like Yitz Greenberg, David Hartman, or Harold Schulweis, my own Jewish path might not have been somewhat different than it has been.

By the time I was a teenager, I had begun to move away from many elements in traditional Jewish practice, for it never occurred to me that these things were connected in significant ways to an "in-depth" kind of spirituality or religiosity. I had not yet been introduced to the writings of Schulweis, Greenberg, Hartman, Kushner, Soloveitchik, Heschel, or Baeck. However, as a senior in college, I was introduced to the writings of Søren Kierkegaard, and I found his work to be the most spiritually and intellectually powerful I had ever encountered. As he spoke about the need for "a leap of faith," I felt that my own spirit, my very soul, was touched. As a result, I had an overwhelming desire to strive to articulate my own understanding and approach to Jewish religious tradition. In a sense, the bulk of my adult life has been spent struggling to acquire a vocabulary to express the most existentially significant commitments I possess, beliefs and practices that define my very being as a Jew within the broader community of humankind.

This process began consciously for me during my senior year in college, when I decided that I wanted to study religious tradition. I was blessed to enter the University of Virginia, where I came under the tutelage of Rabbi Alan Lettofsky. Alan was ordained at The Jewish Theological Seminary and had studied for his doctorate at Yale. He was actually the first person I ever met who was both traditionally observant and concerned with issues of the modern world. I had never met anybody like him in my life, and I remain grateful to this day that at the point when I began to take my Judaism seriously, I had Alan as a guide and mentor. He started me on a path that I have now traversed for more than thirty years.

I could continue with my own autobiographical reminiscences, but I would now like to focus my discussion on the influences of three specific persons: Martin Buber, Mordecai Kaplan, and Abraham Joshua Heschel. These are the thinkers who have given me a vocabulary with which to articulate my sense of Jewish tradition.

As a prelude to my discussion of these men, I would like to share with you a discussion I once had during my teenage years with my mother. I remember asking her, "Do you really think all of the Torah—both Written and Oral—comes from God? And my mother responded by saying, "David, I do not know if every single word in the Bible and Talmud was quite literally given by God to Moses at Sinai. However, I can tell you that if the Bible and Talmud were written by men, it was men who were trying to understand what it is that God wants us to do in the world, so that if God were a human being, God would be happy to be a guest in your home."

I have often thought about my mother's answer as a means of thinking about what is "God-like" or "not God-like" in my life as well as in Jewish tradition. What would it mean to look at Jewish tradition from this perspective? The thinkers I mentioned above have given me a vocabulary with which to attempt to answer this question.

First, the question allows me to see Jewish tradition as an ongoing story in which each generation of Jews writes the current chapter. However, no Jew has to or should start from scratch. Judaism is not a tabula rasa. Instead, each generation writes its own part of the narrative based on and in reaction to the writings that were received from previous generations. There is an inescapable interpretive task that calls on each generation to tell that story and explicate its principles in such a way that, as my mother would have put it, if God were a human being, God would be happy to claim you as a friend.

The question that immediately arises, and that was posed by Spinoza in the seventeenth century, is how can the Bible and Jewish tradition be seen as authoritative if, in fact, human beings authored it. It is not an easy question to answer. However, Martin Buber suggests a way in his philosophy of dialogue. Buber wrote that the irreducible datum of human life is that the nature of what it is to be human is that we live in relationship. Relationship is inescapable, though the nature of relationship is twofold—one he labels "I-It," the other he calls "I-Thou." Note that there is a conjunction between the "I" and the "It" as well as the "I" and the "Thou." For Martin Buber, there is no such thing as a solitary individual. The "I" always lives in relationship—to the world and to others.

The "I-It" relationship, as Buber defines it, is essentially functional. It is purposeful and utilitarian, marked by consciousness and by cognition. An "I-It" relationship is not inherently negative. Buber asserts that the world could not exist without such a form of relationship, and it is in this realm that all of us live most of the time—even with those we cherish most.

However, human beings do not live in the realm of "I-It" alone. Persons possess the capacity to enter the realm of "I-Thou." The "I-Thou" moment of relationship, in contrast to the "I-It," is not marked by consciousness and purpose. Rather, it is defined by immediacy and the overwhelming presence of the other. The "I-Thou" moment is so total and overwhelming that when you are mindful of it you have once more entered into the realm of reflection and "I-It." It is the difference between the moment of immediacy and intimacy that exists between you and your partner and the moment when you attempt to describe that bond of love to another.

Buber's teaching guides my own understanding of Jewish religious tradition and revelation. Buber allows me to define the Bible and the Talmud as expressions of what he labels "I-It" moments. So understood, the Bible and the Talmud represent what might be called love letters. After all, a love letter is not the actual love that exists between two people. In the love letter you cannot possibly exhaust or capture the fullness of the love you have for the other. Instead, you are attempting—with words—to point toward a reality of relationship that transcends the finitude of the moment in which you write and the limitations of the written word. Understood in this way, it is obvious that neither the Bible nor the Talmud literally embodies and expresses the words of God. Rather, they represent attempts on the part of Jews throughout the centuries to point to those pristine moments of "I-Thou" encounters with the Divine. There is an attempt in these literary works to capture the reality of the relationship between God and the Jewish people. When a traditional Jew puts on the *tefillin* (phylacteries) in the morning and recites the words from the prophet Hosea, "I betroth you to me forever," that Jew is attempting to re-create and reaffirm ritually and symbolically the immediacy and the overwhelming power inherent in the relationship between the Jew and God.

The key point that emerges from all this is that our texts and our traditions can be understood as holy even as one rejects fundamentalist claims regarding the inerrancy and immutability of those classical texts and traditions. In addition, Buber teaches about the holiness of relationship itself. Where is it that you encounter God? You encounter God in community. You encounter God in relationships. You encounter God in people.

And this brings me to Mordecai Kaplan. Indeed, Rabbi Kaplan proclaimed an approach to Judaism that speaks to the very core of my being. He taught that you have to look to the Jewish people if you want to understand Judaism. Kaplan loved the Jewish people, and he was both a naturalist and a pragmatist. Theological assertions about the nature of God were less important to him than an analysis of how people actually behave in the world. Does your belief in God cause you to act so that you walk in the world in a God-like way? The real test of how you approach God is reflected through your conduct in the world with other people, not through dogmatic statements about belief. I resonate to Kaplan because my own Judaism is in so many ways "carnal." It is embedded in relationship to the State of Israel, to the Jewish people, and to all humankind.

Mordecai Kaplan was correct about the central role that peoplehood must occupy in an authentic approach to Judaism. For all the theological differences that divide Buber and Kaplan, they converge when they assert that genuine religiosity is discovered in relationships with other people and when they claim that the ultimate task Judaism imposes upon us is to conduct ourselves with loving-kindness in the world.

And now I come to a mystical element in the work of Abraham Joshua Heschel, an element that grants me a language to understand the nature of the world in which we live and the role my tradition assigns my people and me within it. The very title of his magnum opus, *God in Search of Man*, is based on the metaphors of Lurianic Kabbalah, in which, prior to creation, all that existed was God. In order to create the world, God performs an act of *tzimtzum* (self-contraction). God literally contracts into "Godself" and reduces divine being in order for the world to be created. God places the *Shechinah*, God's indwelling divine presence, within vessels (*keilim*) that ultimately prove unable to contain God. The vessels burst, and the world is created in a cataclysmic moment in which sparks of God are hurled throughout creation.

From the standpoint of this metaphor, the universe is "broken," and God, in the very act of creating the world, chose to limit divine perfection. God therefore needs people "to repair the world," and Jews, through the performance of *mitzvot*, "commandments," gather up the sparks of divine holiness that are scattered throughout creation and aid God, serving as partners with the Divine, in the task of *tikkun olam*, here understood as cosmic repair of the universe. This audacious myth asserts that God is in need of each of us if holiness is to be achieved in the world. Our actions have cosmic import. The very presence of God in the world is dependent upon what you and I do. There is a radical religious humanism that is herein expressed. An anecdote about Rabbi Heschel best illustrates this teaching. When I was a boy growing up in Virginia, no ceremony in my synagogue made a greater impression upon me than the ritual of *duchenen*, the ceremony where the *kohanim*, men of priestly descent, would recite the traditional Priestly Blessing upon the congregation. My father would tell me that it was forbidden to look at the *kohanim* while they recited the Priestly Blessing, because the *Shechinah* descended into the congregation at that moment and I would be blinded if I looked at it. Indeed, he even added—as an obvious attempt to impress upon me the gravity associated with a transgression of his instruction—that if I looked a second time, I might actually perish! Even at the age of nine or ten, I said, in response to this warning, "But Daddy, if I looked the first time and was blinded, how would I see the second time in order to die?" At that moment, it was undoubtedly determined that I was destined to become a Reform and not an Orthodox rabbi. In any event, my father did what I now know almost every parent would do in that case. He simply said, "Be quiet and turn around."

I once shared this story with my friend Rabbi Levi Weiman-Kelman of Kehillat Kol Haneshamah in Jerusalem. In response, Levi told me the following story involving Rabbi Heschel from his own childhood in the synagogue of The Jewish Theological Seminary. Levi's father was Rabbi Wolfe Kelman, the executive vice president of the Rabbinical Assembly (the international body of Conservative rabbis). His father, like mine, told him that he was not permitted to look during the ritual of *duchenen* because God's presence would then fill the synagogue. Of course, Levi, like almost any child, promptly stole a glance at the *kohanim* while the ceremony unfolded. He then turned to his father and said, "*Abba*, you told me that I was forbidden to look because I would see God, but instead all I see are men. Where is God?"

Rabbi Kelman then took advantage of a resource my father did not have, for Rabbi Heschel was a member of the congregation. When Levi posed his question, his father did not resort to an "argument from authority," as my father had. Instead, he told Levi that he had asked an excellent question, which should be addressed to Rabbi Heschel. When Levi approached Rabbi Heschel and posed the question, "Where is God?" Rabbi Heschel offered the following response. He said, "Levi, if what you want to do is see God, you need to look in the mirror, but you have to look beyond your face. You have to look deep within yourself, and if you do, you will see that there is a *nitzotz*, a spark of God's holiness, that is there. And when you look at your father and your mother and your sisters, and when you look at all the people you encounter both within the congregation and throughout the entire world, each one is created in the image of God, and there is a spark of holiness present in every single one of them." And Rabbi Heschel then quickly added, "However, the problem, Levi, is that most people forget this truth, and the spark of God that is there remains *nistar*, forgotten and hidden. Your task, Levi, is to uncover those sparks of holiness that are hidden, and you can do this through the performance of *mitzvot*. You take those sparks that are hidden and you make them revealed in the world. You can remind them that they are created in the image of God."

Here we see the power of the kabbalistic metaphor of *tikkum olam*. The way in which you and I behave in the world ultimately helps to shape and repair our universe. At the very heart of our tradition is the notion that there is holiness in the world and that we are responsible, accountable to God, for having such holiness realized. Human beings, marked as we are by frailty and finitude, are nevertheless imbued with such dignity by God that God charges us with the responsibility of contributing to the repair of the world. The notion of covenant reminds us that human beings are capable of "greatness," but not in the sense of power and aggrandizement. Rather, we are capable of displaying care and compassion to one another, and we need one another if the world is to be made a better place.

Passover reminds us of the centrality of this message in our tradition. The Torah commands us not to oppress a person who is "a stranger" and says that we should know the heart of the stranger, the person who is oppressed, because we were strangers in the land of Egypt. The ultimate moral test of a community is to include those who have been downtrodden and forbidden to speak, to give them a voice and grant them the dignity they deserve, because they are creatures fashioned in the image of God animated by holiness. Today, the challenge Judaism poses for us all is one of action: How do we treat our own people, and how do we treat others?

RABBI IRVING "YITZ" GREENBERG

Rabbi Irving "Yitz" Greenberg is the president of Jewish Life Network/Steinhardt Foundation (JLN). JLN's mission is to create new institutions and initiatives to enrich the inner life (religious, cultural, institutional) of American Jewry. Alongside Michael Steinhardt and his son, J. J. Greenberg, *z"l*, he played a founding role in the JLN-initiated partnerships that include such major projects as Birthright Israel, which gives the gift of a ten-day educational trip to Israel to Jews, aged eighteen to twenty-six, worldwide; the Partnership for Excellence in Jewish Education (PEJE), which offers seed money and expertise to create new day schools; and MAKOR (now Makor/Steinhardt Center of the 92nd Street Y), which reaches out to Jews in their twenties and thirties through cutting-edge music, arts, and Jewish educational programs. Rabbi Greenberg also served as chairman of the United States Holocaust Memorial Council from 2000 to 2002. He has written extensively on the theory and practice of pluralism and on the theology of Jewish-Christian relations.

An ordained Orthodox rabbi, Harvard PhD and scholar, Rabbi Greenberg has been a seminal thinker in confronting the Holocaust as a historical transformative event and Israel as the Jewish assumption of power and the beginning of a third era in Jewish history. In his book *Interpreters of Judaism in the Late Twentieth Century*, Professor Steven T. Katz wrote, "No Jewish thinker has had a greater impact on the American Jewish community in the last two decades than Irving (Yitz) Greenberg" (Washington, DC: B'nai B'rith Book Service, 1993). Rabbi Greenberg has published numerous articles and monographs on Jewish thought and religion, including *The Jewish Way: Living the Holidays* (1988), a philosophy of Judaism based on an analysis of the Sabbath and holidays; *Living in the Image of God: Jewish Teachings to Perfect the World* (1998); and *For the Sake of Heaven and Earth: The New Encounter between Judaism and Christianity* (2004).

From 1974 through 1997, Rabbi Greenberg served as founding president of CLAL—The National Jewish Center for Learning and Leadership, a pioneering institution in the development of adult and leadership education in the Jewish community and the leading organization in intra-Jewish dialogue and the work of Jewish unity. Before CLAL was founded, he served as rabbi of the Riverdale Jewish Center, as associate professor of history at Yeshiva University, and as founder, chairman, and professor in the Department of Jewish Studies of City College of the City University of New York.

FROM DESTRUCTION TO REDEMPTION

RABBI IRVING "YITZ" GREENBERG

The years of this generation have been nothing less than the greatest period of Jewish history of all time. Two of the four greatest events of Jewish history have occurred during these eighty years: the Holocaust, a destruction comparable only, perhaps, to the destruction of the Second Temple; and the rebirth of Israel, a redemptive event at least as great as the biblical Exodus. But whereas the biblical Exodus and the destruction of the Temple were millennia apart, the modern events happened in one generation.

What does it mean to be in a generation that opens with an event of destruction greater than any other in Jewish history, followed by the greatest redemption of Jewish history? After the Exodus came the Five Books of Moses—the Torah and the whole Bible is really shaped by that event. After the destruction of the Second Temple came the Talmud. So what will be produced in the aftermath of the greatest destruction of Jewish history and the greatest redemption of that history?

Before we can answer that question, we must first return to the modernization of Jewish life. Jewish life was dominated by modernity because modernity made Jews an offer they couldn't refuse. An old Yiddish proverb says: "Love is wonderful, but love with noodles is even better." What modernity offered the Jewish people was love with noodles. The combination of love (the greatest ideals of all time—human rights, democracy, liberalism, equality, the end of Jewish pariah status) and noodles (economic advance, affluence, a rise in the standard of living, the extension of life) was simply irresistible. And of course, the Jews, in fact, didn't resist.

But although Jews across the board were in favor of modernity, the issue of how, exactly, to modernize was less clear. What exactly does modernity want from us? Each denomination had a different answer to this question.

The Modern Orthodox answer was, "We should speak the language of the country, we should dress a little bit like them, we should give sermons in English, we should not spit on the floor, we should get spittoons ..." In other words, they accepted a new external decorum, but the rest remained the same.

The Conservative position was that to be truly modern, you have to enter into history. Modernity taught us that tradition is also in history, and so one must recognize the change and the growth of the tradition in history.

Reform's answer was that modernity expects us to be rational, to be universal and not tribal. Therefore they decided to clean out those rabbinic traditions that departed from pure reason, the tribal and particularist rabbinic rulings, and the political things that get in the way of the truly universal pure Judaism. By ridding Judaism of these excesses, they argued, and living with integrity by modern standards, it would become the great, leading religion, the light unto the nations.

Kaplan and the Reconstructionists argued that modernity expected a naturalistic God instead of a supernatural Diety, one that was more credible and rational.

Secular Jews said that modernity demanded an end to unbelievable myths, but Yiddishkeit, Jewish culture, and secular Jewish civilization were really credible.

The Bundists and the Yiddishists said that the answer was not just secular culture, but also socialism.

The Assimilationist Jews, or the Communist and Socialist Assimilationist Jews, argued for an end to tribalism, an end to all difference. A single humanity emerges—and if the Jews join humanity, we will live happily ever after.

In short, nobody disagreed completely with modernity. Even the ultra-Orthodox accepted the most extreme claims of the Assimilationists, agreeing that if you accept even the slightest bit of modernity, you have to accept all of it. Therefore, they believed that if one accepts even the slightest bit of modernity, the logical result is total assimilation. That is why the ultra-Orthodox responded by avoiding modern culture as much as possible.

I want to offer my own story as a living example, a case in point of the patterns in modern Judaism. My father was a Litvak and a *misnaged*, a student of Rab Chaim Brisker. He loved Talmud, and he was a *rav* of a *chevra shas* (Talmud circle), teaching Talmud every day of his life, literally, until the last week before his death, when he was too weak.

My mother was a woman of deep elemental piety who spoke to God all the time. I will never forget how on Friday night she would not only light the candles, but have the most intimate conversation of the week with *HaShem* (God), naming each of her children and then each of her grandchildren, and telling God about them, praying for their individual needs.

So I grew up in a home that was saturated with total commitment, observance, and love. I was the last of the children to be born in America, and I am named after my great-grandfather

Yitzchak. However, at my *bris,* when my parents were about to give me my name, they looked at each other and said, "Are we going to name our little child *Yitzchak,* and thereby stigmatize him for life as hopelessly outside the modern American mainstream? No!" They looked around for the most white Anglo-Saxon Protestant name they could find, and they found it—Irving.

My great-grandfather's name was *Yitzchak.* He was named after his grandfather, and so on and so forth all the way back to the patriarchs of the Jewish people, *Avraham, Yitzchak,* and *Yaakov,* not Abraham, *Irving,* and Jacob! So how did I become Irving? I became Irving because my parents desperately wanted to be all-American, all-modern. When it was our turn to name our children, my wife and I revolted against this trend of modernizing. After all, the Talmud says the Jews were redeemed from Egypt because they wouldn't change their names. We felt that a name stood for everything about your values, your belief, your ultimate cause. And so we named our children Moshe, David, Jonathan, Deborah, and Judith. Doing so was a statement of worship. It was a statement of hope. It was a statement of our dream, that we would all become accepted and truly integrated into this culture.

Modernity let the Jews into every new field of education and science, and it was an incredible offer. But in the end, when you change your name, what you're really saying is that it's become a one-way street. The Jewish people were wrapped up in this great dream of joining America and modernity. Why do you think I ended up at Harvard? I was acting out my family's fantasy of Americanization.

The Pittsburgh Platform of 1886 is the climactic, classic document of Jewish modernity. And among its many profound and important statements, paragraph 5 reads: "We recognize in the modern era of universal culture of heart and intellect the approaching of the realization of Israel's great Messianic hope for the establishment of the kingdom of truth, justice and peace among all men." In other words, we no longer consider ourselves a nation, but a religious community, and we expect neither a return to Palestine, nor a sacrificial worship under the sons of Aaron.

Well, a funny thing happened on the way to modernity and redemption. Only it wasn't funny. The Holocaust occurred, in Europe, the heart of modernity, in the most advanced culture in the world, in a country that itself was the high-water mark of science and of scholarship. In the heart of Germany, there was always a party, an individual, who proclaimed that the time had come to separate the Jews, to segregate them, to expropriate and expel them, and finally to exterminate them. All this happened in the heart of modernity.

I once described the Shoah, the Holocaust, this way: "The most total assault of death on the people who teach 'Choose life.'" And the process was death for death's sake. Death defied rational need of wartime productivity, economic profit, or military strategy. There was starvation, disease, terror, deportation, freezing, burning, beating, whipping, live burial, bayoneting, smashing heads, shooting squads, gassing, the Kingdom of Night, and the Triumph of Death.

Of course, the Holocaust was not just a physical assault on the Jewish people, but an attempt to annihilate Judaism altogether. It was a systematic attempt to undermine the central teachings of Judaism, whether they be "Choose life," or the triumph of life, or the value of life. It was a systematic attempt to undermine the concept of *tzelem Elohim*, the image of God in which we are all created.

The Nazis attempted to use Jews to systemically engage in their own self-destruction. They violently attacked Jewish religion. The Warsaw ghetto was established on Yom Kippur,

1940. The deportations to Treblinka started on Tisha B'av, 1942. The final liquidation of the ghetto occurred on Pesach, 1943. These dates are not accidents, not coincidences. They were special roundups scheduled for *yom tovim* (holidays), because the point was to take the holy day, the holiday, and turn it into a day of terror and misery and death.

According to Jewish tradition, you're not allowed to number people; you're not allowed to count them. If you want to have a census, you have to count the number of coins each family donates to represent their numbers. In the universe of the Holocaust, in Auschwitz, you were given a number, and it was prohibited to call you by your name. Both the guards and the prisoners were punished for calling somebody by their name.

The Jewish tradition teaches that the human being is *nivra b'tzelem Elohim* (created in God's image), that every human life has infinite value. That means every human life has infinite value. Saving one life is like saving a whole world. The Nazi counter-testimony is that Jewish life is worth nothing, and you have to reduce its cost. After the war they found an efficiency study that estimated how to maximize the profit of each prisoner—not the ones who were gassed, however, but the ones who were kept alive and worked to death. The study discussed how long they should be kept alive to work, because after a while they become so emaciated and so exhausted they didn't produce as much.

Their ultimate accomplishment came in the summer of 1944, when they were gassing ten to twelve thousand Jews a day in Auschwitz. They complained because the cost of gas was adding up, so someone figured out that you could cut the gas supply in half, doubling the time it takes to kill people in the gas chamber while saving half the cost. And when that didn't bring down the cost far enough, someone finally figured out that if you take the children and throw them directly into the burning pits, you can save the cost of putting them to death. What did it cost them to gas a Jew in the summer of 1944? Roughly two-fifths of a penny per person, based on exactly how many kilograms of gas were used per chamber load of people.

In the summer of 1944, the Pope received reports about Nazi activities. He did nothing. Franklin Delano Roosevelt, the guardian of the Jews, the great president who led us into modernity, whom my parents worshiped because he brought us into the American scene, never lifted a finger.

When Stephen S. Wise, one of the great Jews of the twentieth century, the rabbi who single-handedly brought the Reform Movement into Zionism, heard about what was going on in Europe, he was desperate, and he begged and he pleaded, and he even helped organize a demonstration in New York City. But he didn't get anywhere.

By contrast, in 1943, at the height of the war, A. Philip Randolph, the great African American trade-union leader and the head of the Railway Car Workers, went to Roosevelt and said, "Blacks are fighting in the army; this is a war for democracy. But they continue to discriminate against blacks. The time has come for a Fair Employment Practices Commission." Roosevelt replied that Randolph's request was impossible. The Southern whites would filibuster, and he wouldn't get it through Congress. Randolph protested, arguing for his rights as an American, demanding an executive order. Roosevelt refused, claiming that it would divide the country. So in response, Randolph threatened to organize a march on Washington in which his demonstrators would lie down in the streets, clog traffic, and make such a divisive demonstration that it would tear apart the war effort far more than an FEPC would have. Randolph gave Roosevelt a deadline, and the month before that deadline, he got his FEPC executive order.

So many times I've asked myself why Stephen S. Wise, one of the great Jews of the twentieth century, a Zionist and a passionate lover of the Jewish people, couldn't bring himself to organize a demonstration that would paralyze traffic? Why didn't he do something that would tear the country apart until something was done? Unfortunately, the answer is that Philip Randolph knew, when he looked at his own skin, that he was black and he could never escape that; but Stephen S. Wise, like the rest of the Jewish leadership, really thought he was white. Because all of us were in love with this dream of being accepted and integrated, we didn't fight for our rights as hard as other minorities.

The Holocaust is one of the great devastating, shattering, but also transforming events of Jewish history and, I would argue, of general religious history. First and foremost, it is shattering. I think you have to have a lot of inner courage (perhaps blindness) to go on talking about God after the Shoah. That all three denominations could go on saying the same prayers they said before the Shoah, as if nothing had happened, is shameful. But of course, the issue is not just the shattering. The issue is confronting what kind of religion, what kind of ethics, what kind of life one can speak of in a world in which Jewish children are burnt alive to save half a penny. Do you have a right to raise Jewish children and teach them to be Jews? Is this a form of delusion and dishonesty? Do we have a right to speak of hope? Do we have a right to teach the sanctity of human life? Are we, in fact, making them incompetent to live in the real world? I once wrote that no statement, theological or otherwise, should be made that would not be credible in the presence of those burning children.

What is the consequence of living in this post-Shoah world? We must confront the truth, the revelation of inadequate worldviews. First and foremost, Christianity was judged inadequate. That after two thousand years of Christianization in the heart of Europe people raised as Christians carried out the Holocaust and were not stopped by other Christian people is unacceptable. Christianity set up the Jews, surrounding them in an aura of hatred and degradation, calling them "Christ-killers" and therefore making them exploitable to Hitler. Finally, Christianity was found inadequate by its misdirected protesting. Although there were protests by the Vatican, they were protests only against the murder of Jews who had converted to Christianity. They were pleading, in other words, to save children who believed in Jesus Christ, instead of all children.

Obviously, Christianity is not entirely to blame. Judaism too was found inadequate. Reform Judaism was so blinded by its love of modernity that it became anti-Zionist. How many Jews would have been saved if the Land of Israel had been built up fully a decade or two earlier?

Orthodox Judaism taught passivity. Orthodox Jews believed in God and waited for God to send the Messiah, instead of actively saving themselves. In 1942, when they knew what was coming, when the deportations had just started, Orthodox Jews gathered together to discuss what they should do. Many of the youth movements said the time had come to try to fight, to do something. But Zusya Friedman, the spokesman of Agudas Yisroel, said, "It is prohibited by Jewish law to talk that way. God has always made miracles. We are in danger. This, again, means God will save us with miracles. Anybody who resorts to force will only bring upon us the wrath of the Nazis, and they will destroy us even more. And so it is prohibited in the Jewish law to talk and think in terms of armed resistance."

Rabbinic Judaism said, *Mipnei chata-einu,* "We are punished for our sins in exile," implying that the Holocaust was a punishment for our sins. The Satmar Rebbe said that the sin is Zionism. The Lubavitcher Rebbe said that the Holocaust was God, the surgeon, cutting out the cancer, the gangrenous limb of modernity in the Jewish people. Such a God and such a Rabbinic Judaism is, of course, intolerable and incredible. It, too, is found inadequate.

Finally, modernity itself—that religion that we all worship, that true religion of the Jewish people to this day—made the Shoah possible. Yes, the good side of modernity is totally violated and totally attacked in the Shoah, but how about such fundamental qualities of modernity as bureaucracy? The same bureaucracy that enables us to have Social Security, in which millions of people are categorized and treated equally, made the Shoah possible. As Raul Hilberg points out, when you hate people, you kill them. In the Middle Ages, you stabbed twenty people, or you had a pogrom and killed a hundred people. But when it's done by bureaucrats who write up lists of those to be deported and arranged for the trains, it's a nice nine-to-five, bureaucratically well-done job. As Hermann Himmler said, when he spoke to his officers in 1944, theirs was just a job, just a bureaucratic process.

Value-free science, the glory of modernity, unprejudiced, also made possible people who could be scientific at the expense of human values. The Nazis had great doctors systematically making selections and doing experiments on unwilling subjects in the name of science. This is inadequate. Similarly, the ideological dream utopia—a dream so powerful that it became credible in the modern period—was also responsible. Otto Olendorf, the head of the Einsatz Group, who systematically shot Jews for eighteen months, was the only man who actually admitted to his actions when put on trial. The prosecutor asked him, "How could you do it? Didn't you see the mothers holding the babies? Didn't you hear the screams?" He said, "You know, it was the most difficult thing you could imagine. But I reminded myself what the Fuehrer told us: 'This is the last obstacle to a perfect world.'" That was Nazism—National Socialism.

The horror of the Shoah blinded even the victims. Elie Weisel says that when he arrived in Auschwitz and they came out of this packed car, shocked and stunned, he saw before him an unbelievable, emaciated, horrifying-looking people. Wiesel asked one of the prisoners, "What's going on here?" And the prisoner answered, "You see up ahead? They're going to gas you and burn you." Wiesel, horrified, turned to his father and said, "Father, it can't be. This is not the Middle Ages, this is the twentieth century!" He was one hundred yards away from where they were burning children alive, and yet he was convinced that because it was the twentieth century, the classic age of modernity, such a thing was impossible.

All of those judged inadequate need to be corrected: Christianity, Judaism, science, and utopianism. Modernity, in particular, is the biggest idolatry. Idolatry is when something true, something good, becomes so absolutized as to be seen as all-powerful. Modernity itself was not wrong, but its absolutization, its unquestioned worship, was wrong. That is what made possible the idolatry that turned it into death-dealing and death-supporting instead of life-supporting.

From my perspective, Jewish liberation begins with reclaiming ourselves and our names. I decided, in 1960, when I discovered the Holocaust, to recover myself and my Jewish identity. I began to call myself Yitzchak again. And I decided to become a rabbi again. Until then, I was an American academic historian. I decided to become a rabbi and to give up the title "doctor." In my generation, when a rabbi became a doctor, if you ever called him rabbi again, you lost a friend. So I had to train myself to insist that I wanted to be called rabbi, because rabbi is the superior title. It took months to truly accept that.

How can we talk about God, again, after such an event? My answer is that you *can't* talk about God. You can only re-create the image of God. And if you can re-create the image of God, like you can re-create yourself, that is the statement of God's presence.

After the Shoah, the Jewish people didn't talk about God. What they did was to re-create the image of God. After the war, Bergen Belsen had the highest birth rate in the world. Former prisoners and victims decided to restore the infinite value of human beings by having babies. That's testimony to God.

The UJA responded in kind. They asked people, "Do you believe in the infinite value of *tzelem Elohim* [the image of God]? If so, write a big check." And people wrote million-dollar checks. That's a serious statement about God's presence in the world. Save a Jew anywhere in the world, and you make a statement of the value of life. That is the first step.

To re-create the image of God includes affirming the dignity of equality and the dignity of uniqueness. Personally, I had to ask myself what it is in my tradition that denies the uniqueness or the equality of somebody else. And I woke up, very painfully, to the reality that as an Orthodox rabbi, I was going to have to confront inequality in a tradition that I love. When it comes to women, isn't giving them the equality that they deserve a recognition of their *tzelem Elohim?* What about the uniqueness of gentiles? How do I look at non-Jews?

It's very painful. But if you take it seriously, and if you want to talk about God, you have to take action. That's what the Jewish people began to do when they began to think seriously about these issues.

As part of my reawakening, I joined a Jewish-Christian dialogue, at first because I wanted them to stop spreading hatred and negative images of Jewish people. But soon I discovered that these people are also *tzelem Elohim*, that they have some remarkable capacities for love and for embracing God's presence. Little by little this involvement transformed me to confess the truth—that there were non-Jews living faithfully to their God, and that many of them were doing *t'shuvah* (repentance). They were more self-critical, more willing to transform their religion so that it should stop being a source of hatred and denigration than I had assumed.

From there, I decided to spend less time with them and a little more time with my own tradition, making sure that Judaism, too, stopped spreading negative, hostile images about the *goyim* (non-Jews).

The next step for the Jewish people is to take power. The real issue is not, "Where was God during the Holocaust?" but rather, "Why didn't God stop the Holocaust?" Richard Rubinstein, whom I admire, had the courage to say, "God is dead." But if you don't believe that, what do you answer? I believe the answer is that God was saying, "I am not going to save you." This is *tzimtzum*, divine self-limitation. "I'm asking *you* to stop the Holocaust. You are human, the partner in the covenant. Take responsibility."

What if the Jewish people had heard that message in 1850, and had gone to Israel and built the country then? Millions of people would have been saved. What if the allies had heard that message? In 1935, they could have removed

Hitler for violating the Treaty of Versailles. In 1943, they could have bombed the rail lines.

Taking power is the fundamental transformation of our religion now. We can no longer be a religion that says, "God will save you." God's own message is that you have to take responsibility. If there was ever a time God was going to intervene miraculously, it was during the Holocaust. So if God didn't do so then, God must have intended for us to take responsibility.

The Jewish people overwhelmingly understood that. That's why they arose and declared the State of Israel. Before the war, the majority of Reform and Orthodox were anti-Zionist. After the war, overwhelmingly, the Jewish people became Zionist and understood that taking power is the only way you can live, the only way to combat genocide.

The establishment of the State of Israel was the turning point for Jewish religion and Jewish history. It was the turning point for all of us. That affirmation, that taking of covenantal responsibility, that carrying out of the great redemptive act states, in the face of the contradictory evidence of Auschwitz, that hope is not dead, that life is still stronger than death. This statement—the building of Israel—was done by all Jews.

Beyond the Shoah and Israel, divine *tzimtzum*, that divine self-limitation that said, "You stop the Holocaust. You take responsibility in history," is the culmination of what covenant always intended in the first place. A loving God decided not to force people to be free. That's what the Flood was all about. After the Flood, God took on covenantal self-limitation and said, "I will never again force people to do the right thing. I'm willing to risk their disobedience in order to enable them to do the right thing, freely and voluntarily."

In the Bible, God is still the dominant partner—still very much the one who saves us from Egypt. But if you look at the rabbinic understanding of the destruction of the Second Temple, the Rabbis say God is self-limited. God did not stop the Romans because God is self-limited and invited humans to become full partners in history. Our partnership with God is the reason the Rabbis believed that humans have the power to transform and expand the Torah. It is the basis for the saying, *lo bashamayim hee*, "The Torah is no longer in heaven." We have a major say in what Judaism becomes.

The Rabbis understood, after the destruction of the Temple, not that God had abandoned them, which is what the Christians claim, nor that the enemy was a stronger god, as the Romans claimed. Rather, they understood that God had self-limited in order to ask the Jews to participate. They understood that God is more hidden in our presence, but at the same time, God is in more places—only, we have to discover, we have to bring God out. In this spirit, the Rabbis expanded the scope of halachah (Jewish law) into every aspect of life, bringing religion and purity into the home, so that your meal, your table is your altar.

We are living in the final or third era of this covenant. When God is self-limited, and even more hidden in this world of ours, God is really everywhere. We must have the courage and the insight to discover where, and to explore it.

We are living in the climax of an age that started with destruction and continued with redemption. What is the climax? The climax is nothing less than freedom—the arrival of the potential for freedom. We understand now what it means to be radically free.

On the one hand, we have the freedom to be Hitler, to create hydrogen bombs, to allow evil to wipe out the world, and to allow pollution to destroy the ecology. On the other hand, we can choose to produce enough food to feed everybody in the world, if we have the will to do so. With the arrival of freedom, the great challenge becomes how to show the world to live freely? The Jewish people have exhibited the most incredible power of life itself. In the face of the overwhelming triumph of death, we have not given in, but instead have come back and rebuilt life.

The Jewish people have a chance to show the world that freedom can be turned into human responsibility, mutual love, and accountability. It is the Jewish people trying, again, to teach. To put it into the language of *Shir Hashirim* (Song of Songs), "love is stronger than death." Do not give in to despair, but rather reaffirm life. That's what it means to enter into dialogue with Christians and with Muslims—to learn from them. It means the Jewish people showing the world a model of freedom that leads to a new humility and self-limitation, out of respect for others. It means the Jewish people failing many times, but arising and trying again. That is our unfinished task, the climax we are building toward: to show how freedom and self-development need not turn into narcissism, but into greater human sensitivity and empathy. Freedom can turn into voluntary community and responsibility for people the world over.

RABBI DAVID HARTMAN

Professor Rabbi David Hartman, founder and director of the Shalom Hartman Institute, is a philosopher of contemporary Judaism and an internationally renowned Jewish author.

Born in 1931 in the Brownsville section of Brooklyn, New York, Rabbi Hartman attended Yeshiva Chaim Berlin and the Lubavitch Yeshiva. In 1953, having studied with Rabbi Joseph B. Soloveitchik, he received his rabbinical ordination from Yeshiva University in New York. He continued to study with Rabbi Soloveitchik until 1960 while pursuing a graduate degree in philosophy with Robert C. Pollock at Fordham University. From his teacher Rabbi Soloveitchik, Rabbi Hartman learned that the practice of Judaism can be integrated with a deep respect for knowledge regardless of its source. From Professor Pollock he learned to joyfully celebrate the variety of spiritual rhythms present in the American experience.

After serving as a congregational rabbi in the Bronx, New York, from 1955 to 1960, Hartman became rabbi of Congregation Tiferet Beit David Jerusalem in Montreal, where he had a profound influence on the lives of many of his congregants, some of whom followed him to Israel when he moved there in 1971. While in Montreal, he also taught and studied at McGill University and received his PhD in philosophy.

In 1971, Professor Hartman immigrated to Israel with his wife, Barbara, and their five children, a move that he viewed as an essential part of his mission to encourage a greater understanding between Jews of diverse affiliations—both in Israel and the Diaspora—and to help build a more pluralistic and tolerant Israeli society. It is with this unique vision that he founded the Shalom Hartman Institute in Jerusalem in 1976, dedicating it to the name of his father. At the Institute, Professor Hartman leads a team of research scholars in the study and teaching of classical Jewish sources and contemporary issues in Israeli society and Jewish life. His work emphasizes the centrality of the rebirth of the State of Israel—the challenges as well as the opportunities it offers to contemporary Judaism. His teachings draw upon the tradition of Orthodox Judaism and emphasize religious pluralism, both among Jews and in interfaith relations.

A professor of Jewish thought at Hebrew University of Jerusalem, where he taught for over two decades, Professor Hartman was also visiting professor of Jewish thought at the University of California at Berkeley during 1986–87 and at the University of California at Los Angeles during 1997–98. His involvement goes beyond the academic fields, in which he has published extensively, and his influence has also been felt in Israel's political and educational arenas: from 1977 to 1984, he served as an advisor to Zevulun Hammer, former Israeli minister of education, and he has been advisor to a number of Israeli prime ministers on the subject of religious pluralism in Israel and the relationship between Israel and the Diaspora.

Professor Hartman's publications in Jewish philosophy have received wide recognition and have become standard references in academic scholarship. He was awarded the

National Jewish Book Award in 1977 for *Maimonides: Torah and Philosophic Quest* and in 1986 for the recently reissued *A Living Covenant: The Innovative Spirit in Traditional Judaism* (Jewish Lights Publishing). In 1993, the Hebrew translation of *A Living Covenant From Sinai to Zion* was awarded the Leah Goldberg Prize.

Professor Rabbi Hartman was awarded the Avi Chai Prize in the year 2000, and on the twenty-fifth anniversary of the Shalom Hartman Institute, he was awarded the Guardian of Jerusalem Prize. He was the recipient of an honorary doctorate from Yale University in May 2003. In 2004 he received an honorary doctorate from Hebrew Union College–Jewish Institute of Religion and was awarded the Samuel Rothberg Prize for Jewish Education by the Hebrew University of Jerusalem.

A COVENANT OF LOVE

RABBI PROFESSOR DAVID HARTMAN

The Talmud, in *Sotah*, quotes Deuteronomy 13:15: *Acharei HaShem Eloheichem teileichu*, "You should go after HaShem your God." The Talmud then asks, "How is it possible to go after God? How is it possible to seek God and to meet God and to go with God in life? God is a consuming fire. God is in an overwhelming presence that makes it impossible to seek a relationship." The Talmudic answer is: "Go after the ethical qualities of God." The Bible presents God as a tailor who sews garments for Adam and Eve, as a visitor to the sick Abraham, and as a member of the burial society for Moses. In other words, the Bible's picture of God is one who performs acts of kindness and love. And if one wants to seek, to go after God, one should not look for philosophical abstractions but should rather find a path, an ethical path, that imitates and embodies the spirit of God in the world.

Maimonides' radical negative theology leads in that direction as well. You cannot say who God is, only what God is not, which ultimately means that you can't say anything. To be silent is praise, as Maimonides says. But if this is so, why does Maimonides build the whole notion that love of God is

61

commensurate with knowledge? If knowledge is impossible, then what is the whole foundation of Maimonidean emphasis on philosophical reflection? One discovers this at the end of *Guide for the Perplexed* (3:54 and 3:51), in which a God-intoxicated individual is filled with divine yearning and passionate love. As Maimonides remarks in *Hilchot T'shuvah*, the love of God should be a divine madness, of which the Song of Songs is a parable.

Maimonides guides us toward the knowledge of God's ethical attributes, God's desire to do justice in the world, to pursue kindness. This is what Maimonides understands as the ultimate knowledge of God. To know God is to become a person who lives in an ethical dimension. Ethics is not separated from faith or ritual, but rather it becomes the embodiment of the God seeker.

What we see in the beginning of the Bible is the God of Genesis, the God of creation. God is in total control and experiences this control by creating humanity in God's image and hoping that in this creation, human beings will embody divinity in their life. To God's surprise, the concept of *tzelem Elohim*, the divine image, entails the notion of human freedom. The human being is not a puppet held by the strings of God. The human being is placed in the world to act with freedom and choice. And God discovers that no matter what God does, alone, all God's yearnings for history and for human beings are failures. The story of the Flood, the Tower of Babel, the Garden of Eden, Cain and Abel are all illustrations of the divine experiment and the divine failure to achieve that which God thought God could achieve as the Creator of the world and the all-powerful God of creation.

In coming to realize that God alone cannot bring about the human world that God longs for, God then enters into a covenant with Abraham. God asks Abraham to be a source of blessing for all people—*V'nivr'chu b'cha kol mishp'chot ha'adamah*, "And all the nations of the world will be blessed by you" (Genesis 12:3).

Abraham, as God's covenantal partner, symbolizes a God in need of humanity (or, to use Heschel's language, a God in search of man). This is a God who is not self-sufficient, but a God who comes to appreciate God's own limitations and requires a human partner, beautifully expressed in the covenantal anthropology of Abraham. When God is about to destroy Sodom, God says, *Ham'chaseh ani mei'Avraham asher ani oseh?* "Can I hide from Abraham that which I'm going to do?" (Genesis 18:17). Whenever I meet that verse I say to myself: Why? What does God have to consult us for? He's God! The chief of staff of the army doesn't consult his privates. He gives orders! God gives orders to Noah. God doesn't consult Noah as to whether or not God should destroy the world. God just demands obedience. And yet here God says, "I cannot act unilaterally unless I first consult Abraham." As Rashi points out, before Abraham, God is the God of heaven. After Abraham, God becomes the God of earth. The God of history is mediated by human responsibility.

We know Abraham's famous prayer for Sodom in Genesis 18, which is to me a paradigm of covenantal anthropology. Abraham pleads with God and says, "If there are fifty righteous people, would you destroy the city? God forbid, it's unbecoming for God to destroy the wicked with the righteous. Shall the Judge of all the earth not do justice?" And suddenly Abraham presents a moral critique of God, a moral argument. He doesn't quote a biblical verse. He doesn't say, "I'm speaking in the name of some sort of authority principle." Rather, he speaks on his own moral intuition that it would be unjust to destroy a city if there are righteous people within it. In fact, he demands love—arguing that God should spare the whole city because of the righteous people within it.

As Abraham goes on in his prayer, God could have told him, "Your ways are not My ways. Your thoughts are not My thoughts." God could have overwhelmed Abraham with God's own power and claimed that one cannot use human moral categories to judge God. What we see here is the human being in his moral context, accepted totally by God. To be a covenantal partner is to bring your full humanity into the relationship.

Abraham says, "fifty." And then God says, "I'll spare the city for fifty." Then Abraham goes on to forty, then to thirty. Their conversation begins to sound like the *shuk* in the streets of Jerusalem, a merchant and customer bargaining! God could have told Abraham initially, "Stop your prayers. There aren't ten righteous people in that city." But God doesn't interrupt his prayer. He allows him to go on pleading as if saying, "I love your confrontation with Me. I love a covenantal partner who feels dignified enough to bring a moral critique of My action."

This paradigm of Sodom is called into question reading the text of the *Akedah,* the Sacrifice of Isaac. Here, God asks Abraham to murder his own child, to destroy everything that God promised Abraham, to destroy his future. To kill Isaac is to eradicate the meaning of the future.

How do we reconcile the obedience found in the *Akedah* with the moral critique and confrontation found in the prayer for Sodom? What I claim is that the *Akedah* is not a constitutive principle of Judaism. Rather, the organizing constitutive category from the direction of Judaism is the prayer for Sodom. What the *Akedah* represents is that in living with God as a covenantal partner, the world is not always intelligible. There are going to be moments in which the tragic dimension of life hits you. Are you able to sustain your faith in moments of the incomprehensible? This is the *Akedah*. The *Akedah* is a moment rather than a constitutive idea. We have to learn to live with tragedy and uncertainty as well as with rationality and predictability.

This biblical covenantal principle gets elaborated further when we come to the rabbinic tradition. In the Bible, the covenantal principle is worked through when God says, "Behold, I've given you life and the good and death and evil. Choose life" (Deuteronomy 13:19). In other words, "I give you both paths, but I will not coerce you and tell you how you should live your life. Your life should reflect that which I believe is an important and life-sustaining force. But it is your choice." Covenantal anthropology in the Bible is God abandoning the control, knowing that the only thing God can do is to be an educator. Maimonides understood this well. Revelation is God working with human beings in an educational process. God can educate humanity and bring them to further heights, further growth. But God cannot decide the final step.

When we come to the rabbinic tradition, the concept of covenant deepens. It is now not just a matter of choosing morality or freedom of conscience, but rather a further empowering of humanity to understand the content of revelation. The Rabbis say, "God cannot interfere in the discussions of rabbis in the *Beit Midrash*." The Author of the Bible, the Author of Torah is bound not by God-self, by what God intended, but by what interpreters say it means. The Author does not define the text. Rather, the student of the text makes that decision.

As the Talmud says, *"[Torah] lo bashamayim hee,* "[Torah] is not in heaven" (*Bava M'tziah* 59b, Deuteronomy 30:12). Revelation gives you God's first word, but it doesn't give you the words you live by. I live by not what God said at Sinai, but rather by how the community mediated those words.

In that sense, it is important to understand now what the Rabbis mean by *Torah lo bashamayim hee,* "Torah is not in heaven." When people blame God or the halachah for its moral imperfection, this is a cop-out. Ultimately the halachah is a human institution, mediated by human understanding. It is the human who has to take responsibility for how the Torah gets translated into daily life. So if it gets translated in an ugly, immoral way, then God is not to blame. It's God's covenantal partner who has not used the power and the empowerment that God has given. Covenant is an empowering experience. It is not a submission. It is not a call to unconditional obedience, as Spinoza thought.

Fundamentally, covenants are empowering moments. I become empowered in meeting God. God is not a source of infantilization, as Freud thought, or an opiate for the people, as Marx said. Rather, covenant is a catalyst for human beings to become more empowered to take responsibility.

In the rabbinic tradition, the notion of empowerment is about how to decide the content of Torah. However, history is not defined by human beings, but by God. The empowerment model is limited to the academy of learning. Torah is not in heaven, and when God wants to interfere in the academy of learning, the Rabbis say, "This is not Your place. In the Bible You decided what the law is. Now that You gave the Torah to the community, it is we who decide what the law should be."

There is a very powerful story that is told in *Gemara M'nachot* (29b). Moses asks God if he can visit a future academy of learning, and God grants his request and shows him the academy of Rabbi Akiva. When he comes to the academy of Akiva, he listens to the *shiur,* to the lecture given by Akiva, and the Talmud says that he becomes weak, because he finds that he doesn't understand the discussion. Moses, the giver of

Torah, does not understand the discussion of Rabbi Akiva with his students, and he becomes deeply depressed. "How is it that the Torah, which I gave, becomes unintelligible to me when my students are interpreting it?" He becomes comforted when the students ask Akiva, "How do we know this law that you're talking about?" And Akiva answers, *Halachah l'Moshe mi'Sinai*, "It is the law that Moses gave at Sinai." Ironically, although he doesn't understand the discussion, Moses is comforted by the fact that his name and role in history are remembered. Then Moses asks God of Akiva, "*Zu Torah*, this is his Torah—tell me his reward. Tell me his condition in history. What does he gain and benefit given his great dignity and great creativity in the academies of learning?" So God shows him a barrel of cut-up meat, which was the body of the martyred Rabbi Akiva. Moses then goes to God crying out, *Zu Torah, v'zu s'charah?* "Is this the Akiva I met in the *Beit Midrash*, the Akiva of such great dignity and strength and intellectual powers? Hanging in the street like a barrel of dog's meat?" And God answers Moses's protest: *Sh'tok*. "Be silent. This was my decree."

In the academy of learning it's the Rabbis who say to God, *Sh'tok!* "Be silent. Thus is my decree. This is what you gave us. This is the Torah that we are responsible for. So therefore, God, be silent in the academy of learning!" But when we leave the academy of learning, when we leave this rational, intellectual world, we meet a God who tells us, "Silence!" before the incomprehensibility of history.

The paradigm for Jewish history has always been the paradigm of the Exodus from Egypt. The Exodus from Egypt in my theology is again one in which God is the sole actor in history. God breaks through because of God's promise to the patriarchs and because God hears the suffering of God's people. The liberation from Egypt was an act of supernatural grace. It was God's breaking into history and giving history a new direction of freedom.

As long as that paradigm operated in Jewish history, Jews waited with courage for the coming of the Messiah. They felt their suffering in exile would end only by a supernatural act of divine grace. Then along came the Zionist revolution. Many people think that Zionism is a rejection of the tradition. To me, Zionism and the creation of the State of Israel are a new expression of covenantal empowerment. What the Jews decided is: Exile will end when we take responsibility for history. We have to learn banking. We have to learn agriculture. We have to learn self-defense. Only through our initiative will there be a change in Jewish homelessness.

We have, then, three aspects of the covenant: the covenant of the Bible, the covenant of the Talmud, and the covenant of contemporary Jewish history in Israel.

People often ask me, "And where is God for you?" If God is neither the source of the law, nor the source of history, what is God's role? And the only way I can understand this is that God now becomes the Covenantal Presence. God is not a function. God doesn't bring about anything. What God does is bring about something of the empowering of human beings, so that they don't abandon their ability to assume responsibility. God is the energizing principle for a deep moral and social activism within the community.

The covenant of presence is the covenant in which what you seek from God now is not some teaching or some sort of liberation. What you seek from God is not that God will solve any problem, but that God should be with you. As an example, when my father died, I missed him terribly. I missed the warmth of the *Shabbos* table and his song, and I often wished he could be with me again, not because I wanted him to solve my problems, but because I wanted him to be present to me. I wanted to feel the joy and comfort of being in the presence of my father. The deepest dimensions of love are not necessarily functional, utilitarian relationships. The deepest dimension of love is to say I seek Your presence.

Therefore, for me, the spiritual moment in contemporary Jewish history is a covenant of love. Here, reward and punishment cease to be an operative category for me. Reward and punishment cannot work anymore in the modern world, because we have other forms of gratification and other ways of creating obedience to the law. God is now sought not because of a function but because God is God.

If you ask me what functional meaning I would give to this category, I would say that what God means for me in the modern world is that I don't have to try to fool myself, to become perfect and absolute and God-like. To know that I'm only human, frail, full of weaknesses, is what is achieved by positing a transcendent God. God is Other. Not me. Sartre is concerned that if God is Other than man, man cannot be dignified. To me, the very Otherness of God empowers me to accept myself in my weaknesses, in my frailty, in my finitude. God allows me to be human and doesn't demand of me to make myself God.

RABBI HAROLD KUSHNER

Rabbi Harold Kushner is rabbi laureate of Temple Israel in the Boston suburb of Natick, Massachusetts, where he served the congregation for twenty-four years. He is best known as the author of *When Bad Things Happen to Good People*, an international bestseller first published in 1981. The book has been translated into fourteen languages and was recently selected by members of the Book-of-the-Month Club as one of the ten most influential books of recent years.

He has also written *When All You've Ever Wanted Isn't Enough*, which was awarded the Christopher Medal for its contribution to the exaltation of the human spirit. In 1995, Rabbi Kushner was honored by the Christophers, a Roman Catholic organization, as one of fifty people who have made the world a better place in the last fifty years. His other books include *When Children Ask about God, Who Needs God, To Life*, and a 1996 bestseller, *How Good Do We Have to Be?* With novelist Chaim Potok, *z"l*, he is coauthor of the new Conservative commentary on the Torah, *Etz Hayim,* which has been enthusiastically received by hundreds of congregations since its publication in the fall of 2001. His most recent books are the best-selling *Living a Life That Matters* (2001) and *The Lord Is My Shepherd: Healing Wisdom of the Twenty-third Psalm* (2003).

Rabbi Kushner was born in Brooklyn, New York, and graduated from Columbia University. He was ordained at The Jewish Theological seminary in 1960 and awarded a doctoral degree in Bible by the seminary in 1972. He is the recipient of six honorary doctorates, has studied at the Hebrew University in Jerusalem, and has taught at Clark University, Worcester, Massachusetts, and at the Rabbinical School of The Jewish Theological Seminary. For fours years, he edited the magazine *Conservative Judaism*. In 1999, the national organization Religion in American Life honored him as their clergyman of the year.

ENCOUNTERING THE LIVING GOD

RABBI HAROLD KUSHNER

What has happened to the American Jewish community in this generation? How have we changed, and how have I changed?

Ours was the generation that saw the American Jewish community come of age and mature. I hold in mind two parallel moments. The first was in the 1940s, during the Second World War, when a delegation of rabbis and American communal leaders went to see Franklin Delano Roosevelt to plead with him to do more to save the Jews of Europe.

The rabbis, many of them born and educated in Europe, many of them speaking with accents, were so over-awed by this patrician, articulate, charismatic Ivy League–graduate president, so overwhelmed that the president of the United States had found time to speak and to listen to them, that they almost failed to notice that he didn't promise to do anything to aid their cause. That was 1942.

In 1967, when Israel was endangered on the eve of the Six-Day War, once again, a delegation of American rabbis and contributors to the Democratic Party went to the White House to meet with President Lyndon Johnson. And in 1967, it was the rabbis who were the Ivy League graduates, and the president who spoke with an accent. This time, they did not beg. They demanded.

We were a more confident, secure community by 1967. The establishment of Israel had a lot to do with that. The maturing of our community had a lot to do with raising the profile and the pride level of American Jews.

Will Herberg, in his book *Protestant, Catholic and Jew,* broadcasts what happened in the period between the Second World War and the suburban explosion. In the 1930s and 1940s, Jews were marginalized and insecure, echoing the words of Abraham in the Torah, who said to the children of Chet when he tried to buy a burial plot from them, *Ger v'toshav anochi imachem,* "I am a resident alien, a stranger among you" (Genesis 23:4). The Rabbis interpret this to mean: "I'm not sure if I belong here or if I'm just visiting. I'm not sure if I have the right to be here, or if I'm just here on the basis of your tolerance."

By the evolution of the Protestant-Catholic-Jew triad in the 1960s, we'd outgrown that insecurity. For fourteen years I had a weekly radio program in Boston. We would tape it on a week-day afternoon, and it would be broadcast at six o'clock on Sunday morning. It was a typical panel for those days—a priest, a nun, a Protestant minister, and myself. If you tried to run a program like that today, the Evangelical Christians would say, "Hey, wait a minute! The Episcopal minister doesn't speak for us." And the Unitarians would say, "There has to be a seat for us." And the Mormons would say, "What about us?" And the Muslims would say, "We're almost as numerous as the Jews." And perhaps the Hindus and Buddhists would claim their space as well. Can you imagine the joke that begins, "These twelve clergymen walk into a bar ..."?

But for several decades, we Jews were 3 percent of the American population and 33 percent of the religious panels. We had transformed America from a Christian nation into a

Judeo-Christian culture. What happened during those decades is that the American Jewish community began to produce its own scholarship, and that made all the difference.

Rabbi Arthur Hertzberg, an eminent colleague and a very fine historian, theorizes that during the massive wave of immigration from 1881 to 1924, the millions of Jews who came to America from eastern and central Europe were mainly the ambitious, young, rootless, unmarried people with no means. The scholars, wealthy storeowners, and landowners stayed behind in eastern Europe and perished in the Holocaust.

Those who came to America were people with a sense of Jewish identity but little Jewish knowledge. So in the 1910s and 1920s the American Jewish community was large in numbers but largely uneducated. Their Jewishness, the original American Jewishness, became an undifferentiated blend of authentic Judaism and Polish superstition—and nobody knew which was which.

By the 1950s, children of uneducated parents became uneducated parents themselves. Nobody knew what was going on in the American Jewish community. And then, through some mysterious resurgence of the life force, we began to come back.

The building in which Harold Schulweis and I studied, The Jewish Theological Seminary in New York, was at the forefront of that shift in consciousness, training authentic, homegrown Jewish scholars and sending them out to populate not only the synagogues, but the universities of the United States. This was the beginning of a Jewish community that wanted to learn, a community that found its own teachers.

The same thing happened in Los Angeles. The establishment of the University of Judaism transformed West Coast Judaism, making it much healthier, more confident, more rooted.

Beyond that, the generation spanning the years of the 1950s, '60s, and '70s was the generation that had an amazing impact on American culture. Many people find it hard to believe that Jews make up only 2 percent of the American population. They're convinced it's mathematically impossible. After all, everybody's doctor is Jewish. Everybody's lawyer is Jewish. Everybody's accountant is Jewish. Everybody's favorite comedian is Jewish. Andrew Heinze wrote a book called *Jews and the American Soul,* in which he argues that American Jews shaped American identity in the twentieth century. At a time in the early twentieth century, when the impact of immigration caused Americans to wonder about their identities, along came Sigmund Freud, Erik Erikson, and other psychoanalysts, almost all of whom were Jewish. They invented the concept of the identity crisis, the sense of the unconscious. Jewish analysts helped Americans understand who they were. Their theories have become so pervasive, in fact, that we can't even remember what it was like not to think in Freudian terms.

As Americans became more urban and moved from the countryside to the cities, they looked to Jews to teach them how to be city dwellers, because we were city dwellers before them. As Americans worried about the impact of all these social changes on their families, they looked to the American Jewish community to teach them what it meant to be a family. As Americans tried to understand the world around them, they turned to the writings of Bernard Malamud, Saul Bellow, Philip Roth, Chaim Potok, and Isaac Bashevis Singer. The movies, from the beginning, were almost entirely a Jewish industry, capturing Jewish dreams of what it means to be an American.

This acceptance, which made us comfortable and bought us admission to the best neighborhoods and universities and to the highest levels of American society, came with a price. As we were accepted, we assimilated and increasingly began to intermarry.

Soon, assimilation became a crisis for the American Jewish community. Today, some people worry about it, while others panic. My advice for decades now has been a very simple one. You want to know what to do about the intermarriage crisis? See it as a doorway *into* the Jewish community, not a doorway *out*. Maybe in the 1930s, the Jew who wanted to marry a non-Jew was looking to escape Jewish identity. But Jewish identity is not that sort of burden today. Being Jewish is "in"; it's attractive and exotic. All we have to do to solve the intermarriage problem is make the non-Jewish partners feel welcome in our midst—in our synagogues, in our community centers, in our homes.

So, why don't we do it when it's such an obvious solution? Perhaps it's because there are a lot of us who still aren't sure that being Jewish is a good thing. And we're really not sure why anyone in his or her right mind would want to be Jewish if they didn't have to be. You know the jokes we tell about ourselves: How do we know that Jesus was Jewish? Because he was thirty years old and unmarried and lived with his mother, who thought he was God.

There are jokes about Jewish mothers, and jokes about Jewish American princesses. Is it any wonder that people aren't quite sure if we want to entice people to become part of us? And yet it not only solves the intermarriage problem, but solves all sorts of problems. Talk to any congregational rabbi in America, any one, and he or she will tell you that when it comes to conversion, our imports are superior to our exports.

Our congregations have been enriched by the accession of people who are not born Jewish. When I spent eight years editing the *Etz Hayim* Torah commentary, I was surprised to find the wealth of favorable comments in the rabbinic tradition about the desirability of converts to the Jewish people, about the eagerness of the traditional rabbis to welcome converts. No one teaches these sources, but it seems to me that's exactly what we need to do.

What has this generation done for the Conservative Movement? My parents had a friend back in Brooklyn, New York, who had served in the United States Army during the Second World War. He liked to joke, "I don't want to take all the credit for myself. All I know is when I joined the army we were losing the war, and by the time I left we had won."

My take on the history of the Conservative Movement is, when I entered The Jewish Theological Seminary to study to become a rabbi, Conservative Judaism was the strongest, most dynamic movement on the American Jewish scene. By the time I retired from the rabbinate, thirty-five years later, it was failing and shrinking and losing its energy. And I don't want to take all the credit for the change.

What happened? One reason for the shift was that there was something very strange in the air as the twentieth century yielded to the twenty-first—the moderate center was eroding. Not only in Judaism, but in Christianity and Islam as well, the extreme movements were gaining strength as the center was eroding.

This same trend is happening in politics. It seems to be a very difficult time to be a moderate in anything, because we are living in a time where a lot of people are searching for certainty. I think it was President Clinton who said, "In times of uncertainty, there are many people who will follow a leader who is confident but wrong, rather than one who is tentative but right."

It is the nature of a liberal, moderate person to be tentative, to refrain from saying, "I'm right and everybody else is wrong." But there are a lot of people out there who need and crave that sense of certainty, and it's hard for us, sometimes, to give it to them.

Another strange thing has happened to the Conservative Movement as well. When I entered The Jewish Theological Seminary in 1955, the chancellor, Dr. Louis Finklestein, was a Talmudist, a brilliant student of rabbinics. And the Conservative Movement defined itself as a historical movement. In the year 2005, the chancellor of the seminary was Professor Ismar Schorsch, a historian, and we're defining ourselves as a halachic movement.* I'm not sure how that happened. Nobody asked me. I don't remember ever voting on it. But I suspect it was a mistake.

As Conservative Jews, it is history that validates us. It is history that validates our right to make changes in how one practices one's Jewish identity. I will not accept the notion that Conservative Judaism is for people who don't have the nerve or the devotion to be Orthodox, or for people who are too lazy to do "real Judaism."

I will insist that Conservative Judaism validates itself because of its sense of history. When we chose to ordain women as rabbis, when we voted to permit women to be called to the Torah and to read from the Torah, we didn't do so because we were desperate to lower the standards and increase the number of rabbis. It's not because we were following the secular culture or because we didn't care about Jewish precedent. And it's certainly not because we found permission in traditional halachah to do it.

What we appealed to was history. In the biblical period and in the rabbinic period, it made sense to differentiate

*Editor's note: The Jewish Theological Seminary subsequently named Professor Arnold Eisen, a scholar of Jewish intellectual history, to succeed Chancellor Ismar Schorsch.

between the private roles of Jewish women and the public roles of Jewish men. In the twenty-first century, however, it makes no sense at all. In a world where women had no public role, understandably, they would have no public role in the synagogue.

In today's world, where women are senators and Supreme Court justices and CEOs of major organizations, how can anybody try to justify that sort of gender segregation within the synagogue? It is history that validates us. It is history that permits us to say, Jewish law has always changed, as circumstances changed.

I was lecturing once at a synagogue in Virginia. And in the question period somebody asked me, "Rabbi, my neighbor says to me that only the Orthodox will preserve Judaism. Do you think she's right?" And I said, "Yes, absolutely, she is correct. Only the Orthodox will preserve Judaism. They will preserve it the way you preserve jelly. You put it in an airtight container and don't let the outside world in."

Jewish law has always changed. That's why it was always relevant. That's why people were loyal to it. That's why people studied it. Not only to know what has been done, but to know what should be done. And it seems to me that this is where Conservative Judaism should be drawing its identity and its strength. That's how we have changed.

As to how I have changed personally, I can tell you not only how I've changed, but when I changed. I can tell you the exact moment when my perception of what it meant to be a believing Jew changed abruptly.

On November 20, 1966, a doctor told my wife and me that our three-year-old son, who had not been growing normally, would never grow normally. He suffered from an extremely rare disease called progeria, rapid aging, which would keep him very small and strange looking and would ultimately cause his death in his early teens.

I don't have to tell you what something like that does to a person. What made it even harder for me to hear the doctor's words was when I tried to say to myself what I as a Conservative congregational rabbi had been accustomed to saying to congregants. I discovered with a shock that the words I'd been taught to say were not comforting.

To say that we can't understand God's ways, but ultimately this will be for the best—no, that didn't work. To be told that a religious person should never question God—that didn't work either. I was very angry. I was angry at God and I was angry at Jewish tradition, and I was angry at the teachers who taught me to use those words and persuaded me that I would be comforting people when I said them.

I went through a severe crisis of faith, trying to make sense of the doctor's decree. What saved me was going back to the Bible, reading the book of Job, and finding an answer there that I had never found before. What saved me was reading an essay by Archibald MacLeish, who wrote the play *J.B.*, the book of Job in modern setting, which led me to the conclusion that not everything that happens in the world is the will of God.

Why did it ever occur to us that God wanted children to be born deformed? Why did it ever occur to us that God wanted the young mother to be stricken with multiple sclerosis? That God wanted the young husband and father to fall dead of a heart attack? Where did we ever get the notion that we add to God's glory by holding God responsible for every earthquake and tsunami, every hurricane and forest fire, every landslide, every automobile accident, every terrible disaster, including the Holocaust?

Some traditional critics have challenged me, arguing that the God I describe is a weakling. I don't think that's true. But even if it were, there are worse things than being a weakling, and one of them is being a child murderer.

Once I cut the Gordian knot, I understood that God was not doing this to my child. God was on my side, not on the side of the illness. God was on the side of good people, not on the side of the people who victimized them. God was on the side of the Jews who died in Auschwitz, and, God forbid, certainly not on the side of their oppressors.

Once I understood, as the Protestant theologian David Ray Griffin likes to say, that although God is all-powerful, God's power is not the power to control, it's the power to enable, I could go back to God again. And I could see God as responsible for giving my wife and me the strength—and for giving our son the strength—to cope with all the things we had to cope with.

For those of you who have read or will read my most recent book on the Twenty-third Psalm, that's the message I find there. Rabbi Schulweis's and my mentor Mordecai Kaplan used to say, "Expecting the world to treat you fairly because you're an honest person is like expecting the bull not to charge you because you're a vegetarian."

Reluctantly, very reluctantly, we all come to understand that life is not fair. We don't want to hear that message. We would rather believe that somebody is driving the bus. We would rather blame ourselves and tell ourselves we deserve it than admit that some things happen in the world at random.

Do you know why we respond the way we do to the prayer *Un'taneh Tokef* on Rosh Hashanah? Do you know why we give it prime space and get more emotionally responsive to that than at any other moment of the service? Because that's what it says to us. It says to us in the first part of the prayer, the part about the record being in our own handwriting, that half of the things that are going to happen to us in this next year are the results of things we have done—what we ate and how we lived and how we've carried things out—it is our responsibility.

And then the second part of the prayer says, *B'Rosh Hashanah yeikateivun*—it is decided on Rosh Hashanah and confirmed on Yom Kippur who shall live and who shall die, and there's nothing you can do about it.

It is unsettling to be told that things will happen that are not fair and there's nothing you can do about it. But ultimately, we gain nothing by hiding from the truth. And the truth is that life is unfair. The truth is that the role of God is not to weave a magic circle around us and make sure bad things happen only to other people. The role of God is to strengthen and to comfort. The role of God is to be with us. That's what God's name means—the One who is with you. The role of God is to hold our hands and, when we find ourselves in the valley of the shadow of death, to take us by the hand and lead us through the valley, till we come out into the sunlight again.

Martin Buber once made a distinction between theology and religion. He said, theology is talking about God, religion is experiencing God. And, he said, the difference between them is the difference between reading a menu and having dinner.

Theology can be enlightening. Theology can be informative. But theology cannot nourish the soul. Only the encounter with a living God can nourish the soul.

When the psalmist, the author of the Twenty-third Psalm, is living in a world of sunshine and green pastures and still waters, he talks *about* God: "He makes me lie down in green pastures, He leads me beside the still waters." It's only when he is cast out of the sunshine, into the valley of the shadow, that he makes the transition from theology to religion. Instead of "*He*," the psalmist now says, "for *Thou* art with me."

He discovers that the reality of God is not a God who controls, and not a God who justifies, but a God who comforts.

My son's illness changed everything for me. And in the process of sorting out my new theology, I found Rabbi Schulweis's concept of predicate theology immensely helpful. When I try to explain it to people who have never heard the phrase before, I like to tell the story of the time David Ben-Gurion, then prime minister of Israel, went on a European trip to try and sell Israel bonds and raise some money for the state. He was introduced to the wealthiest Jew in Antwerp, a diamond merchant. He entered the man's sumptuous office. The man said, "Mr. Prime Minister, before you start I want you to know something. I consider myself a human being first, a Belgian second, and a Jew third. Does that offend you?" And Ben-Gurion said, "No, not at all. In Hebrew we read from right to left."

That's predicate theology: taking all the things that our tradition says about God and reading them from right to left, so that all those statements are not biographies of God or descriptions of what God is, but descriptions of what God does.

After one of my lectures, a woman approached me. "My ten-year-old son says he doesn't believe in God," she said. "How can I persuade him to believe in God?" I said, "Wrong question. Firstly, you can't talk anybody into believing in God, especially a ten-year-old. And besides, that's not the purpose. Jewish education is not about teaching people to believe in God. Jewish education is teaching people to recognize God when they have met God."

I used to tell the Hebrew teachers in my synagogue religious school that on the day of the first snowfall in the winter,

I didn't want to hear that they called the kids away from the window back to page 46 in the book. The response of a young child to that first snowfall is as religious an experience as anything in a lesson plan.

Predicate theology is teaching Jewish children to recognize the presence of God in the beauty of the world on a nice day, and to recognize the presence of God in their own ability to heal when they are sick and in that good feeling that quivers inside them when they share their toys with another child. God, too, is present in the miracle of being forgiven when they have been caught doing something wrong. Predicate theology is not asking, "Where is God?" or "Who is God?" but "When is God?" "What are the moments in which we can find God present?"

The other great lesson I've learned from Rabbi Schulweis is that "Why me?" is not a question. "Why did this happen to me?" "Why my family?" "Why my father?" These are not questions. They are cries of pain. And the authentic Jewish response to the person who says, "Why me?" is not to answer her question, but to ease her pain.

At some level we intuitively know this. When your best friend says to you, "What did I ever do to deserve this?" she really doesn't want you to tell her all the things she's done to deserve this. When a person asks at a more serious level, "Why is this happening to my family?" the last thing in the world she will find comforting is to be given all the reasons why this is happening to her family. I have learned to explain less and to hug more. I am absolutely convinced that when I do that, I am incarnating the presence of a loving God, who does not justify misfortune and unfairness, but tries to give us the strength to live through it.

I look back at my decades in the rabbinate, and what have I learned? People ask me if I think the human race is getting better or getting worse. And I say, "Yes." We're getting better *and* we're getting worse. I would like to think that incrementally we are getting better.

In just one lifetime, we have seen the defeat of Hitler, the fall of Communism, the establishment of Israel, the repeal of racial segregation, the empowerment of women, the extension of the life span, and the eradication of all sorts of diseases. It should give us reason to look forward to the rest of the twenty-first century, to get even better.

PART II

THE COVENANT, THE COMMUNITY, AND THE FUTURE

When the Talmud's students wondered whose opinions of Jewish law should prevail, those of Hillel or those of Shammai, a voice came down from heaven and announced, *Elu v'elu,* "These and these are the words of the living God." Dialogue is the authentic expression of Jewish truth. In dialogue there is room for divergent opinions and alternate interpretations. Perhaps in the heavens, God speaks in monaural. By the time the divine voice reaches us, it is heard in multiple voices.

Ideas matter. These five rabbis—Ellenson, Greenberg, Hartman, Kushner, and Schulweis—have contributed ideas that have transformed Jewish life in the late twentieth century. Our discussions focus on their ideas and on the ideas that will shape Jewish life in the coming century: pluralism in the Jewish community, our message to the non-Jewish world, the new spirituality, the meaning of the Holocaust and the State of Israel, our hope for a revival of Jewish life.

For these five rabbis, ideas are not cold abstractions but the product of their passionate engagement with the agonizing Jewish experiences of the twentieth century—the experience of a community split and torn, the internal brokenness of Jewish community life and narrowness of Jewish vision. Like our ancestor Jacob, they have wrestled and they have prevailed. At the end, they stand hopeful and excited about the prospects for a new Jewish century. And like Jacob, they bear wounds, but they bring blessings.

ON THE ROLE OF THE SYNAGOGUE AND RABBI IN TOMORROW'S JUDAISM

RABBI FEINSTEIN:

Rabbi Kushner and Rabbi Schulweis, you are both synagogue rabbis with very distinguished careers in congregations. There are those who study the American Jewish
community and believe that the synagogue has no future,
that as an institution it has outlived its time, and that the
time has arrived for some other institution to take its
place. What is the power of the synagogue and the congregational rabbi, and what is their future?

RABBI KUSHNER:

I think the synagogue offers a couple of unique things
that cannot be replicated any place else. It offers community in a very special way.

We live in a world that works so hard to separate old
from young, rich from poor, successful from less successful. Los Angeles, for example, is a very hard place to live
for a woman who is not attractive and a man who drives
an old car. The synagogue is the one place in town where
those distinctions are not permitted to enter. This is the

one place where everybody is equal, where nobody counts as more than one for the *minyan*, where everybody is welcome, where nobody's trying to sell you anything.

When the Conservative Movement reluctantly decided to accept driving to synagogue on Shabbat, they did so because they understood that technically you could stay home and read the prayers and study the Torah portion by yourself, but by doing so you miss the essence of what it's all about.

I myself go to *shul* partly to hear a good sermon these days, but primarily to be with people whose lives I want to be a part of.

The second thing that the synagogue offers us is something that you cannot find anyplace else in the city, and that is holiness. The synagogue is a building dedicated to sacred moments. There are people who will come and remember that they were married there. There are people who will come and remember that they and their children became bar or bat mitzvah there. There are people who will come and remember that they *benched gomel* there when they came out of the hospital.

There is a sense of holiness, a sense of finding something in a synagogue that I could never find anyplace else. In the *Etz Hayim* commentary, at the very end of the book of Exodus, I talk about how the Jews at this point are left with the holiness of time and the holiness of place—the holiness of presence and the holiness of encounter.

There are moments in life when God suddenly erupts into our lives. When you fall in love, when you get married, when you become a parent, when you're saved from danger. Those moments are unpredictable; you can't order them up. And then there are moments when you want to capture that sense, but you're not getting married or being saved from danger that day, so you go to the synagogue, and you remember what it feels like to be in the presence of God.

RABBI SCHULWEIS:

I honestly believe that the synagogue is the most important, significant, and potentially revolutionary institution in Jewish life.

Harold Kushner and I are synagogue rabbis. I think what appealed to us is the "ought" that we got from Kaplan and from Heschel. The question is not, "What is the synagogue?" The question is, "What ought the synagogue to be?" The question is not, "What is a Jew?" The question is, "What ought a Jew to be?" The question is not, "What is a rabbi?" The question is, "What ought a rabbi to be?"

If you think in terms of the normative, rather than descriptive, you will see the synagogue with its tremendous potentiality. I have found my synagogue to be an opportunity to deal with what I consider the major concern of Judaism—to cultivate in all of us a conscience, a moral sensibility. That expresses itself in all of our activities. A rabbi can speak nobly, but unless there are people out there who pick up his or her talk, it simply becomes vapid and ephemeral. So the synagogue is primarily an opportunity for a culture of conscience.

Secondly, the synagogue incorporates the three things that Kaplan always talked about: belonging, behaving, and believing. We know that we're not alone when we come to *shul*. We know because we have a common concern, a common belief, a common behavior.

Lastly, the synagogue is a therapeutic institution. When I feel depressed, when I feel worried, when I

become terribly self-centered, and I come to the synagogue, I look into the eyes of other people, and I feel a
tremendous healing of the spirit. There is no institution
that has greater promise to give joy and to transmit wisdom to world civilization than the synagogue.

RABBI FEINSTEIN:

For the Jewish community of tomorrow, what do rabbis
have to know? Who do rabbis have to be? And what
quality would you want of these rabbis as they begin
their leadership in the Jewish community of tomorrow?

RABBI ELLENSON:

In my current capacity, I think a great deal about this
question that you've posed. In a sense, we have a traditional formula that speaks to us in regard to these issues.

In the Sephardic tradition, a rabbi is often referred
to as *marbitz Torah* [one who spreads Torah], at other
times as *chaver* [friend, scholar], and also as *chacham*
[wise person].

The very essence, the foundation of being a rabbi
has to be knowledge of Torah. What absolutely distin-
guishes us from other persons who engage in other pro-
fessions is the knowledge of Torah that we carry with us.
Consequently, it strikes me that whether we're talking
about rabbis a hundred years ago, a thousand years ago,
or today and in the future, there has to be a very sound
textual foundation upon which all of us build, as well as
a historical, philosophical context.

Simultaneously, a rabbi has to have a sense of empathy for the people whom she or he serves. Unless you are
able to internalize the notion of *al tadun et chavercha ad
shetagia limkomo* [do not judge another until you've

stood in his place] and you can feel what the other person feels and have a sense of what the person's needs are, you cannot exercise effective rabbinic leadership and pastoral care, nor can you facilitate people through their crises of life. Hence the need to be a *chaver* [a friend].

And finally, what does it mean to be a *chacham* (a wise person)? The task, which confronts all of us, is to be aware that we live in conditions that are radically distinct from those of our ancestors. Just as we're anchored in the roots of our tradition, we also have to be cognizant of what the demands of our day are. If we consider North America alone, the traditional associational and kinship patterns that mark our community have radically changed as we move into the twenty-first century. Consequently, our ability to reinterpret and understand our tradition in ways that will reflect the wisdom of that tradition allows other people to see the beauty inherent in Judaism as they anchor themselves in the Jewish community and then move out into the larger world. All of these qualities remain prerequisites for rabbinic leadership.

RABBI KUSHNER:

We're familiar with the term *baalei t'shuvah,* those who have returned to Judaism. I think the rabbis of tomorrow have to be *baalei she'elah* [those who have questions]. They have to know what questions animate our congregants. The genius of Harold Schulweis is not simply that he is smarter or more learned than anyone else, but that he hears people's questions. He invented the *chavurah* movement because he heard the loneliness of the family that had to sit shivah alone when their nearest blood relatives were two thousand miles away. He brought his theology of relationship into the congregation because he heard the existential loneliness of the person who felt no relationship to God.

When I try to write a book, once I can clarify what question I'm trying to answer, the book is half written, because I know where to find the answers. When we were rabbinical students, we were given answers. We spent class after class hour, year after year, course after course being given answers, and the implicit message was: "If these answers don't fit your congregants' questions, educate them to ask the right questions. Teach them that they should ask you whether Sweet'n Low is pareve, and not how to find meaning in their lives."

If we're going to be effective, we have to hear the questions, and that, it seems to me, is that task to which we have to devote ourselves.

RABBI GREENBERG:

In the end, Judaism—the religion a rabbi is trying to teach and to communicate and to transmit—is about creating a perfect world. That's what *tikkun olam* means. What's the definition of the perfect world? I would argue that in Judaism it means it's full of life, because God loves life, especially life in the image of God—human beings, in which all the dignities of *tzelem Elohim* [God's image] are honored and respected, including infinite value, equality, and the uniqueness of every human being.

Now, how do you go from a world like ours to a world where everybody is treated with infinite value or equality or uniqueness? The Jewish answer is that you create mini-worlds in which people experience the messianic, and then you go back to the real world and you try to transform it to fit that model. So where is this mini-world? The *Beit Hamikdash* [the Holy Temple] was such a place. It was a world untouched by death, where theoretically nobody was hungry and everybody got justice, where God's presence was felt because you felt the full humanity of every human being. Shabbat is a remnant of that world. On Shabbat, you live in a perfect world, where there's nothing left to be done and you can experience the full human relationship, the full spirituality.

What a rabbi tries to do is to create these mini-worlds, to bring people within them and then simply reach out and expand them. On Shabbat, in the *shul*, the rabbi creates a space in which *tzelem Elohim* is fully respected. In the synagogue, everyone feels infinitely valuable and equal. Their unique pains and joys are shared and respected and honored in that space.

The rabbi's role is to teach this idea so the rest of the world can believe in it. When you see slavery or cruelty or war, you don't believe that the world could ever be perfect or that everyone really has a dignity of infinite value. But when you teach someone that that ideal exists, you change their world. Not only does the rabbi teach this, he or she must also be a personal role model. The most important contribution a rabbi can make sometimes is to show people how to love, how to be a parent, how to be a friend, and how to really care when somebody's crying or laughing. A rabbi's contribution to the congregation is not simply how much time is spent in the office, but how he or she acts as a human being.

Another role for today's rabbi is to be a coworker. Jewish people are not going to save the whole world alone; they need others' help. And the rabbi's not going to create the perfect world alone, because such a thing is impossible. Recognizing that you can't do it all alone is the first step. Then you have to recognize that you don't need a *shul* to make an impact. You can influence people in community centers, camps, schools, and even factories.

RABBI FEINSTEIN:

If a young person comes to you and says that he or she wants to be a rabbi, would you approve of that career choice?

RABBI KUSHNER:

It depends on the young person. If the person is suited, I will tell him or her that during the many years I was a congregational rabbi there was nothing else I wanted to do with my life. I was absolutely delighted, and I felt very privileged. I had college classmates who were making more money than me. And I had college classmates who had more spare time than I did. But I went to bed every night knowing that I had made a difference in people's lives, and that there were people who were lost, and I helped them be found. There were people who were scared, and I gave them courage. There were people who were depressed, and I gave them hope. And there were people who were floundering, and I gave them a sense of direction.

The Shabbat that I retired from my synagogue in 1990, the congregation had a dinner in my honor, and they asked me say something. I took my text from *Birkat Ha-mazon*, the Grace after Meals, where we ask that God bless us as God blessed our ancestors, Abraham, Isaac, and Jacob—with a *b'rachah sh'leimah*, a complete blessing.

"Now," I said, "if you go back and read the stories of Abraham, Isaac, and Jacob, you might wonder how blessed they actually were! Quarreling with their wives, conflicts with their kids, and so on. Maybe a *b'rachah sh'leimah*, a complete blessing, doesn't mean only the good things. Maybe it's the blessing of wholeness."

It seems to me that a rabbi, more than any other profession, experiences the wholeness of life. A rabbi will celebrate a bar mitzvah on Shabbat morning and counsel people on Shabbat afternoon. A rabbi will go from an unveiling to a wedding, will see people at their best and at their worst. A rabbi will understand the range, the breadth, and the depth of life, and will have the opportunity to do something about it.

There are very few people, no matter how much money they make, no matter how nice a house they live in, who can look at their working lives and know that they have done that.

ON THE LEGACY OF MORDECAI KAPLAN

RABBI FEINSTEIN:

Rabbi Kushner and Rabbi Schulweis, you were both students of Mordecai Kaplan. His message shaped and molded the American Jewish world in the 1950s and the 1960s. As we enter this generation, it seems that his message is eclipsed. What is enduring in Kaplan's teaching?

RABBI KUSHNER:

Let me start with the part that's ephemeral. I was a student of Kaplan in the 1950s. My mother was his student in the 1920s at the Seminary Teacher's Institute. The Kaplan that my mother talked to me about when I was growing up was a man who looked at a Jewish community and saw people who wanted to do Jewish things, if it could be made intellectually acceptable to do so. And he designed a Judaism for people who couldn't imagine eating non-kosher, couldn't imagine not going to synagogue on Shabbat. He just wanted to tell those people that they were not being medievalists by wanting to hold onto their traditions.

99

We don't have people like that anymore. We don't have people who hesitate before they leave a lot of Jewish tradition behind. What is enduring in Kaplan is the notion that the Jewish people and the Jewish community is permanent. Forms and rituals and theologies can change, but Judaism is still Judaism.

I believe one of the fundamental structural differences between Judaism and Christianity—not a theological difference, but a structural one—is that we were a people before we had a faith. Christianity, on the other hand, was a faith before it had a people.

So Christianity rests upon its theology. When you stop believing what the authorities tell you to believe, you have to form a new denomination. Judaism rests on the community. You start a new *shul* if you don't like the rabbi and the president of the one that already exists in your town.

It is that sense that we are a family, and not a political party, that permits us to differ sharply and still know that we belong to each other, to change and to change radically, and to know that we are still lineal descendants of Abraham, Isaac, Jacob, Akiva, Hillel, and Maimonides. I think that, for me, is the central idea Dr. Kaplan taught me.

RABBI SCHULWEIS:

Mordecai Kaplan was not "theologically correct." When I graduated from Yeshiva College in June of 1945, the *New York Times* had a banner headline that read, "Orthodox Rabbis Burn Rabbi Kaplan's Siddur." I had never heard of Mordecai M. Kaplan, so I certainly didn't know he had written a Siddur. And I began to read about Kaplan, and read his Siddur, and I realized that this was hot stuff. In fact, when I went to Kaplan and I asked him how he felt about the burning of his Siddur, he said, in the optimistic spirit, that things were getting better. In the time of Calvin and Servetus, the heretic was burned. Now they only burn the prayer book. Not bad.

What was unique about Kaplan for me was one of his favorite quotations from Ahad Ha-Am. He said that in Hebrew, if you want to say, "I was," you say, *ani hayti*. If you want to say, "I will be," you say, *ani ehyeh*. If you want to say "I am," you say just *ani*. There is no "am." There is no present tense in Hebrew. And that is what Kaplan meant for me. There was in Kaplan a respect for the present tense. Kaplan was the only one of the faculty, and they had wonderful people on that faculty, who asked a different kind of question.

He would ask his students, for example, "Do you believe that women are inferior to men? Do you believe that women ought not to be called to the Torah? Do you believe that women ought not to be counted in the *minyan*?" And everybody said, "Of course we don't." And his next question was, "What are you doing about it? Do you believe that if a *kohein*, a Jewish priest, wishes to marry a *ge'rushah*, a divorced woman, or a *gioret*, a proselyte, that they should not be allowed to be married?" And they said, "We don't know. It says so in the Bible." But he said, "What do you say? Please don't give me quotations. Don't tell me what Abaye said. Don't tell me what Rava said. Tell me what you yourself say." And that shook up the group.

When I taught classes in contemporary Jewish philosophy at Hebrew Union College and the University of Judaism, I would always ask those kind of questions. "What did Leo Baeck say about resurrection? What did Maimonides say about sacrifices?" And then the last question was also, was always, "And what do *you* say?" That was the hard question. So what Kaplan did for me was to indicate that I was not simply a passive "amen" sayer, a link in the tradition. I was responsible to improve and strengthen the links of my tradition.

RABBI FEINSTEIN:

Kaplan's contribution to Jewish theology was to try to free Jews from personalist language about God. I'm interested in your take on that idea. In your books, Rabbi Kushner, you refer to "the Living God." Rabbi Schulweis, you and I have sat next to each other on the *bimah* for these many years, and I know that when you *daven*, you *daven* to Somebody. I want to understand how we're to talk about God.

RABBI KUSHNER:

First of all, I love Mordecai Kaplan. He saved my life, Jewishly. He taught me how to understand being Jewish and how to be a rabbi. But God bless him, he wrote with a pen dipped in cement. He had no sense of poetry.

He was so serious about the urgency of saving Judaism that he had no room for anything trivial. I remember Dr. Kaplan talking to us about the Jewish meteorologist who puts on *tefillin* in the morning and, after he says *Sh'ma Yisrael*, reads the next paragraph about how if the Jews are observant then God will send rain, and if not, not. He then takes off his *tefillin* and goes to his job and does not make his weather forecast on the basis of Jewish behavior.

Kaplan asked, how could a man be so inconsistent? How can he be such a hypocrite? If he doesn't believe in something, he shouldn't say it in his prayers. Kaplan simply could not understand poetry. And I think he felt the need to take a lot of things out of Judaism because he couldn't appreciate the poetry of it. He wanted to replace *Kol Nidre,* because he felt it wasn't believable.

When I pray, as a disciple of Kaplan, I think of God as a person to whom I am praying. And then I tell myself, this is *my* limitation. I know God is not a person, but I simply don't know how to think of God in any other way. All of those references to the sight of God and the hand of God and the outstretched arm of God—yes, they're poetry. And you don't take a poem literally.

I think of God as a person, but I know God is not a person, just as I speak of sunrise and sunset although I know that the sun isn't really rising and setting. There is no word, there is no translation to express what God is. There is no definition of God, because to define is to limit, and I'm not about to do that.

What do I mean when I say I believe in a personal God? I don't believe in a physical being, a Michelangelo muscle-bound bearded old man who lives in heaven. I believe God is personal in this sense. Some physical forces, like gravity, are impersonal. They treat us all the same. If you fall out of a building, you will head toward the ground accelerating at a certain rate, irrespective of who you are and why you're falling.

But then there are forces like love and courage, which treat every individual differently. One person will have more courage than another in certain circumstances. One person will be motivated by love in a situation where someone else is not. One person will have a stronger sense of honor and obligation than another person.

God is personal in that sense. God operates differently in my life than in yours or in theirs. In that way, the One God is a personal God.

RABBI SCHULWEIS:

It is correct that prayer is poetry, but it is poetry *believed in.* It's not just pretty. It's not just aesthetically pleasing. It has to be something that you honestly believe in.

We say the prayer, "who shall live and who shall die," and then the prayer says, "prayer and repentance and charity will avert the severity of the decree." Does this mean to tell me that God decreed the death of my child? Or the death of my father? Kaplan was very serious and said, "If you are going to say it, you've got to believe it." Most people, I'm convinced, believe that prayer literally just as they believe the prayer, "because of our sins were we exiled from the land." They believe it literally, not poetically.

If you don't translate poetry into a prose that people understand, you risk their misunderstanding. This is the case with the confusion about the words "personal" and "person." I believe in Godliness, but I do not believe that God is a person. I never believed that God was a person, any more than I believed that Santa Claus was real. But I do believe in the predicates, the gerunds of prayer. In order to believe, I must express my belief behaviorally—in loving, in caring, in being concerned, in lifting up those who are fallen, in healing those who are sick, I express Godliness. And I don't need a God-as-person for that. When I suffer, who comforts me? Who consoles me? You do. My people do. When they come to the home, when they come to shivah. That is called Godliness. Does God console me and comfort me? The answer is yes. Through you.

RABBI KUSHNER:

Menachem Mendel of Rymanov said that human beings are God's language. God responds to our outcries by sending us people.

I agree, but I would add one idea. I would defend to Dr. Kaplan and to anyone else the legitimacy of reciting prayers you don't believe. There is merit to the *matbea shel t'filah* [the traditional order of the prayer service]. There is merit to our all reading the same prayer on the same page at the same time, and not having a cacophony of individual meditations.

Something magical happens when we are singing and chanting together. You transcend your individuality and you become part of a greater whole. And for that we've all got to be saying the same words, whether we affirm them or not.

RABBI SCHULWEIS:

As Conservative Jews, we've changed those prayers. We no longer pray, "Blessed art Thou, Lord our God, who has not made me a *goy* [non-Jew]." We no longer pray, "Blessed art Thou, *Adonai* our God, who has not made me a woman." So this argument fails in that respect. Some things I can't pray.

RABBI KUSHNER:

Agreed. My answer has always been that when a prayer offends me, I want to change it. Like the examples you gave. However, when a prayer contradicts my theology, I have no problem reciting it.

ON THE NEW SPIRITUALITY

RABBI FEINSTEIN:

There is, in the culture now, a powerful sense of spirit, an interest in spiritually, and a search for religious experience. What do you make of these trends? What do you make of the search for religious experience? What is its value, and what are its dangers?

RABBI KUSHNER:

In the last few decades, we have discovered that the best and the brightest don't know how to get us where we want to go. We have discovered the limitations of a strictly intellectual, rational approach to life. We have discovered that there has to be more to life than what makes sense. And so we are looking for the nonrational.

You will remember that one of our most prominent and beloved and cherished professors at seminary used to say, apropos of mysticism: "Nonsense is nonsense. But the history of nonsense is scholarship." Our school was dismissive of anything that was not rational.

And the result is that the authors of liberal Judaism in this country threw out everything that they could not justify and understand rationally, and then found themselves undernourished. I once compared that to lifting the hood of my car and throwing out everything the function of which I did not understand.

As a result, liberal Jews were confronted by a Judaism that spoke to the top three inches of their head and ignored the rest of their body. It is not surprising that some turn to Buddhism, and some turn to the Unification Church, and some, thank God, turn to Chabad, which I think of as the Starbucks of Jewish life.

The most important things in life don't make sense, such as our decision about whom to marry or where to work. Choosing whether or not to tell the truth in an embarrassing situation. Those are not rational issues. Those are emotional issues. And, for God's sake, a religion that insists on making sense is such a narrow religion that it will leave people emotionally malnourished.

RABBI SCHULWEIS:

I think there has to be greater warmth, and it seems to me that Chasidism introduced that warmth. But what frightens me is what Dostoyevsky described as the things that people desperately want, things they are willing to sacrifice their morality and their intellect to get: People want magic. They want authority. They want authoritarianism. And they want it now.

As a Jew, I come from the tradition of Maimonides, of the Bible itself, and of the rabbinic tradition that fought so hard not to allow oneself to become sucked into quick, shortcut magic.

A woman once came to me with a book called *The Zohar* and said that it cost her $450. I said to her, "Do you read Aramaic?" And she said, "No." "Well," I asked, "what did the rabbi who sold you that book tell you about it?" She answered, "He said to open up the book, put my finger on the line, read across it, and voila." That is superstition. I don't think that I want to be part of a tradition that sells itself out for that kind of magic.

RABBI KUSHNER:

If people don't get that sense of wonder, that sense of transcending the rational (not irrational, but trans-rational) in *shul*, they're going to get it in all these misbegotten places. And it's our fault. It's our fault for not realizing that we have to feed their souls and not just their minds. My parents were both Litvaks. They come out of that staunchly intellectual tradition with scorn for the Chasidic ways of jumping up and down and getting drunk and all of that. And it took a lot to liberate me from that Litvaksha [Lithuanian rationalist] tradition.

Jack Bloom's thesis is that the average congregant sees his or her rabbi as a symbolic exemplar—that a *Mi Shebeirach,* a prayer for recovery from illness, recited by the rabbi is more potent than one recited by the relatives of the individual or by some other employee of the synagogue. Bloom is saying, "Don't fight it, use it." If people believe that the rabbi has priestly powers, don't waste your energy telling them that a rabbi is just a Jew who's gone to a school for more years. Use the magic. I'm ambivalent about it. How do you respond to it?

RABBI SCHULWEIS:

My congregation will never make that mistake. They know that their rabbi is fallible, that he or she does not know the answer to a lot of questions. I spend a lot of time convincing people that I cannot pray for them. I want them to pray for themselves, but I will pray with them. I'm worried about the manipulation, the religious leader who will say, "I'm not saying this, I'm not curing you, I'm not healing you ... God is, through me."

RABBI FEINSTEIN:

So, if there is this impulse in the community toward spiritual experience and spirituality, and at the same time there is a sense in the culture at large of extremism of all kinds, do you believe that liberal Judaism has a future?

RABBI KUSHNER:

It had better. I think that's authentic. I think it meets the genuine needs of people. Robert Frost once said that he wished he could be king of an island where true ideas go when they're out of fashion, so he could take care of them until they're rediscovered.

I feel like I'm a custodian of some of those true ideas. I will continue to advocate them, and continue to preach them, and insist on them until this Kabbalah fad wears off and people come around to ask for what we have to dispense.

RABBI SCHULWEIS:

Different things move us. What moves me most, in Judaism, is the reality principle. There is a section in the Bible, a remarkable section, in which the Jewish people are being poisoned by serpents. God says to Moses, "I want you to make a brazen serpent." Then it says, in the Bible itself, that when the people look at the *n'chushtan,* the brazen serpent, they are healed. Now that's the end of the Bible's story. But there's a rabbinic tradition that asks how a brazen serpent can make a person whole. What happened to the magic serpent? The Rabbis say that when it became an object of worship, King Hezekiah destroyed it, and he was praised. That's what moves me.

I don't want magic. I don't trust magic. I come from a tradition in which there are no shortcuts to truth, no shortcuts to love, no shortcuts to belief. Beware of this chicanery, this manipulative magic.

ON THE ROLE OF
DENOMINATIONS

RABBI FEINSTEIN:

I think it was Yitz Greenberg who was quoted as saying,
"It doesn't matter what you are, Conservative,
Orthodox, or Reform, as long as you are ashamed of it."
What is the future of our denominations?

RABBI GREENBERG:

This is a true story! I gave a talk at the RCA [Rabbinical
Council of America, organization of Orthodox rabbis] in
which I tried to argue that in the Shoah no denomination
showed any particular capacity to understand what was
happening, to deal with it, or afterward, to properly
change their behavior. When I got through, somebody
got very angry, jumped up, and said, "How dare you say
that? What are you really saying? That we're all the
same? So what should you be after the Shoah? Orthodox,
Conservative, or Reform?" To which I answered, "It
doesn't matter which one, as long as you're ashamed of
it." And of course, he got twice as enraged, and he yelled
at me, "So why are you Orthodox?" I said, "That's the

group I'm most ashamed of." That was the last time they asked me to speak at the RCA.

I have always said that it's okay to have denominational loyalty, but you must also have loyalty to *Klal Yisrael,* to the Jewish people in general. You have to be willing to criticize yourself in order to gain credibility. When you criticize the other, there's always an element of defensiveness about it. But if you criticize yourself, it means that you have integrity. Paradoxically, self-criticism evokes the response of the other, who must learn to criticize themselves. One of the problems in Jewish life is that each one can give you a long list of what's wrong with the other denominations.

It was only when I met Harold Schulweis and people like him that my life was transformed, because I suddenly recognized in myself that inherent arrogance. I really thought that Orthodox rabbis automatically were smarter, more learned, more observant. It was tremendously liberating, chastening, and humbling for me to meet Jacob Petuchovski and realize he was a Reform rabbi. As a *talmid chacham* [learned man], he had come to the conclusion that certain *halachot* [Jewish laws] were morally inadequate and needed correction. When I overcame my arrogance and self-flattery, I realized he was right. I was so busy feeling superior to the Reform that I couldn't admit it before.

When I met people like Harold Schulweis and Seymour Siegal and realized that their spirituality and passion, their commitment and observance and integrity were at least as good as mine, it really liberated me to listen to why they were different and to learn from it. Even if I didn't accept it, I learned from it and learned to respect it.

RABBI FEINSTEIN:

Rabbi Ellenson, you work for a denomination. Of all of us, you are the most identified with a denomination. What's the role of denominations, and what ought to be the role of denominations?

RABBI ELLENSON:

One of the great difficulties that we all confront is quite simply sitting down and being with one another. There's a real danger in having a world where people, in fact, don't talk across denominational lines. The ability to caricature and stereotype one another becomes infinitely more complex when you know given individuals.

My own experience has been that the stereotypes people guard can be so overwhelming that even when they meet the other individual, that other individual becomes the *yotzei dofen*—the exception to their stereotype. I often say that knowing only one or two things about any topic is enjoyable, because that way reality need never conflict with my prejudices in any way, and I can see things, as it were, much more simply.

The denominations are an interesting phenomenon to me, and I speak here in part not simply as someone who heads a Reform seminary, but as someone who has been a historian of these enterprises and who has lived within different denominational settings virtually my entire life.

Denominationalism is really only a phenomenon of the last two hundred years. That's not to say that there were not Pharisees, Sadducees, Karaites, and Rabbanites in past ages. But in reality denominationalism arose as a variegated way for different groups of Jews to respond to the challenge of what it meant to be Jewish in the modern world.

It is interesting to note that Germany did not have the kind of denominational divisions that exist in the United States today. There was an Orthodox community and a liberal Jewish community. Graduates of The Jewish Theological Seminary in Breslau (a traditional seminary) and graduates of Abraham Geiger's *Hochschule* (a Reform seminary) actually joined the same rabbinical body. People like Leo Baeck and Hermann Cohen, persons who we see as paradigms of Reform Jewish teaching, attended The Jewish Theological Seminary in Breslau. Abraham Joshua Heschel and Solomon Schechter attended the *Hochschule* in Berlin as well.

Of course, part of the reason why that was possible is that the level of observance in German Judaism was much more similar and, I would add, traditional than it would be in an American setting. The Orthodox religious seminary and the liberal or Reform, the *Hochschule*, were on the same street in Berlin, and the students all attended classes together at the University of Berlin. They came to know one another *panim el panim*—face to face. They were friends with one another. They weren't common cultural types. In the United States, we had a split between eastern European and German Jews. What we call in America Classical Reform Judaism really was the first religion of Jews of Germanic descent in America, created at the beginning of the twentieth century. Conservative Judaism, on the other hand, came to be the folk expression of people of eastern European descent.

The denominations do stand for something, and there are certainly theological differences among them. But while significant today, they are not as crucial as they

once were in previous generations, when the socioeco-
nomic differences that confronted the Jewish people in
America made them so decidedly different from other
Americans. The reality is that we have a common
Jewish community out there. What I wish we could
bring about in the Reform Movement would be greater
Jewish literacy. But the reason why there is not greater
Jewish literacy isn't simply because of the Reform
Movement. It's the sociological reflection of who and
what Jews are in the American setting today. And it
strikes me that these are common problems, common
sets of concerns that all of us need to confront.

I would argue that we need to understand that at the
same time as we attempt to strengthen Jewish life in this
country for that committed core who have renewed their
Judaism in virtually unparalleled ways, with greater
degrees of knowledge, depth, intensity than would have
been true in my parents' generation, simultaneously there
are millions of Jews who are crying out for our leadership
and support. They're asking us in a very real sense to
facilitate their entry into Jewish life. The issue is how to
make them into serious Jews. And here the modeling and
all the other points that my colleagues have made today
come to be so crucial. I do think that we may be at the
beginning of a transformation or change in which
denominations may disappear, but we will come to
understand that that which unites us as Jews may be
more significant in terms of the questions we confront
than the differences that separate us.

One rabbinic quote comes to mind. There was in
Germany an Orthodox *Gemeinderabbiner*, a community
rabbi. He didn't serve a separatist Orthodox congregation,
but in Germany, in Frankfurt, there was a community of

a *Gemeinde* structure. So the rabbi could serve the entire community. One of the rabbis there was named Anton Nobel, who later became the teacher, among other people, of Franz Rosenzweig.

At the beginning of his career, Nobel was asked how he saw his mission as a rabbi. And he said that while there were causes that separate us, he chose *l'hadgish et hakav hame'ached otanu,* to emphasize those factors that unite us. And it seems to me that we are at a time in Jewish life when the ultimate challenges that confront us are present across boundaries and borders.

It is interesting to me to note the number of "intermarriages" among graduates of the Hebrew Union College and The Jewish Theological Seminary and the University of Judaism! That is not insignificant. I say it in some ways like a joke, but the shame of all of this is that we won't see many such marriages between graduates of Chovevei Torah, much less Yeshiva University and those from The Jewish Theological Seminary or Hebrew Union College, or the Academy. What that speaks to in terms of *Klal Yisrael* is one of the ultimate divide that I do feel marks our people as we move into the twenty-first century. But it also testifies to the permeability that exists in virtually every other sector of the Jewish people today. After all, when people marry one another, they usually take one another—I hope—fairly seriously.

RABBI SCHULWEIS:

Why has denominationalism or congregationalism kept us apart? Why is there so much apartheid in Jewish life? Why do our children not pray together? Or play together? Why is it in fact the case that we have divided a people and created all of these stereotypes: The

Orthodox are crazy. Reform are lazy. Conservatives are hazy. They may be right, but there is something wrong here. There's something very wrong here. We cannot afford this type of denominational divisiveness. We cannot afford the fact that our people don't get together. I don't understand why a gathering such as this one should be unique.

I was raised in New York. Yeshiva College was on 186th Street and Broadway. At 122nd Street was The Jewish Theological Seminary. A little further down, just a subway stop or two, was the Jewish Institute of Religion. Do you know that in all my years in the seminary, no Conservative rabbis, myself included, went to hear Yosef Baer Soloveitchik. And no Orthodox *yeshiva bocher* heard Mordecai Kaplan or Abraham Joshua Heschel. And none of us heard Harry Orlinsky. There's something wrong with us, and in order to correct it I think we have got to begin by saying, we're not going to allow the denominations to destroy our sense of *Klal Yisrael* [the unity of the Jewish people].

Mordecai Kaplan used to say that denominational Judaism is like keeping traffic. The green light is the Reform Movement, signaling, "Go right ahead." And then there's the Orthodox Movement, which is like a red light saying, "Stop." And with the Conservative Movement, it's a yellow light, telling us, "Go with caution." So a Conservative Jew is considered to be one who has never tried to do anything for the first time.

A number of years ago, I introduced a thing called "The Best of Judaism." What we had was a series. One was "The Best of Satmar." Next was "The Best of Lubavitch." Then we had "The Best of Conservative," "The Best of Reform," "The Best of Orthodoxy." The topic of these talks was, "What is it that appeals to these people?" As I believe Rav Kook once said, you can overcome *sinat hinam*, causeless hatred, with *ahavat hinam*, causeless love. We have got to be together. And our congregations have got to be together. This is very, very important.

ON ORTHODOX AND NON-ORTHODOX JUDAISM

RABBI FEINSTEIN:

The element of the Orthodox community that would share this sort of a conversation is small. Rabbi Greenberg, is there some way for Orthodox Jews and non-Orthodox Jews to talk to each other, or are we rapidly reaching the point when we are in fact two separate religions?

RABBI GREENBERG:

Of course we can and must talk to each other, and thank God there are places like Hillel, where you have an opportunity to meet Jews of every denomination. I'm happy to say that there are Orthodox rabbis around the country who participate in this kind of conversation. That having been said, you touch a very painful sore point here. In 1984, I published a piece called "Will There Be One Jewish People in the Year 2000," in which I argued that we are turning into two peoples. Today, the issue has quieted down and generally people are positive about the state of the Jewish people, since we don't seem to be fighting like we fought twenty years ago. But the truth is that we aren't fighting because we are so separated. And I grieve about that. I do not think that people realize this catastrophic reality.

Recently, a woman called me with a problem. She had been married by a Conservative rabbi, a good personal friend of mine, and was now about to marry an Orthodox Jew. She had received a Conservative *get* [religious divorce] from her first husband, but her new rabbi didn't want to acknowledge the validity of her Conservative *get*. Because I know that the rabbi and the *beit din* [religious court] who performed the *get* were very learned and observant, they were hoping that I could help. How? They had heard a rumor that this Conservative rabbi who had performed the original wedding was not *shomer Shabbat*. If I would testify to that rumor, they could then say that the original marriage was not valid, so that the validity of the divorce would not be an issue. In other words, it was easier halachically and communally for them to say that a Conservative rabbi is not *shomer Shabbat* and therefore invalidate a marriage than it was to acknowledge a Conservative *get* that was done properly.

The fact is that there has been a rupture at a very deep level. And for the moment, this is the way the majority of Orthodox communities seem to be headed. I'm not asking for pity, but my position is isolated, relatively marginalized. The majority of the Orthodox Jews agree with me, but they are not calling the shots in the actual process of the community and its halachic and communal institutions. The opposite is happening. And I find it extremely depressing.

In 1984, after my articles on Christianity, there was a heresy trial. And one of the charges made against me was that pluralism is relativism. I was said to be teaching that there is no difference between Conservative, Orthodox, and Reform, as well as between Judaism and Christianity. To this day, this charge frustrates me, because the difference between pluralism and relativism is the fundamental difference we all have to learn. Relativism means that anything goes, which is a moral and spiritual disaster. But pluralism means we have real differences. We disagree, but we have limits to our truths, and those limits make room for somebody else's truths, even contradictory truths.

I'm an Orthodox rabbi, an Orthodox Jew. I'm almost ashamed of it, because, as one so deeply invested in Orthodoxy, the flaws, weaknesses, intolerances, and arrogances of the movement upset me more. When Reform misbehaves, I feel bad, but it's not my community in the same way, so I feel less pain. When Buddhists misbehave, I feel even less pain. But with the Orthodox world, it's very painful for me, very direct.

When I started exploring other communities, my first step was to go to other services, but not *daven* [pray]. I *davened* in the morning first and then went to the other *minyan*, because I felt that I wasn't being halachically fulfilled there. Only when I met the reality of the living communities and I experienced them did I realize that I felt the presence of God and I felt the presence of *minyan* and community. I realized I could be *yotzei* outside of an Orthodox *shul*, fulfilling my religious obligations there.

When I am in a Jewish community where I can't take an *aliyah*, I experience it as a living example of the pain of exile. To me it feels like the *Kadosh Baruch Hu* [the Holy Blessed One], the *Shechinah* [God's presence], is in *galus* [exile], and I'm in exile as well. The fact is that passionate, committed, observant, learned people think that the only way that they can ever hold their truth is by denying the spiritual truth of the Conservative and Reform Movements. It's a tragedy for them.

On the other hand, although I don't want to simply justify the Orthodox, there are liberal Jews who should ask themselves how they contribute to this environment where genuine, sincere people feel that the only alternative they have in upholding tradition is by denying the other. It's a good experience for everybody. I have seriously considered not taking an *aliyah* in an Orthodox synagogue, too, particularly as I continue to experience the reality that women can't get an *aliyah*.

My final comment is that you can't quit. We have to approach each other again and again. Rav Yisrael Salanter tells the following story: He once came to a rich man, who gave him money three times for the poor, and he said, "Don't come again. I've given enough. I'm never going to give money again. I'm tired. Don't bother coming back anymore. You've asked me too many times." The rabbi raised as much as he could, but he still needed money. So he went back to the fellow a fourth time. The fellow got very angry, and he said, "I told you not to come here." The rabbi said, "I had to ask you. There's no money. The poor need it." The rich man got so angry that he slapped the rabbi in the face. When he got through the slapping, Rabbi Salanter said to him, "Well, that's what you have for me. Now what do you have for my poor people who still need your help?"

I'm not asking Conservative and Reform Jews to be slapped again. But I would urge them to go back again and discuss that "slap," that dismissal, that arrogance. And then ask, "Now what do you have for me? What do you have for *Klal Yisrael* [the Jewish people]?" You have to approach them again and again and again. That's the real measure of who loves *Klal Yisrael*. Never mind the speech that we love the Torah, we love all the Jewish people. Practice talks louder than the words. So go back again. Because somehow, maybe with your love and your kindness, you will win them into a new conversation, which will release them from prison and help them become true *Klal Yisrael*.

RABBI SCHULWEIS:

Yitz Greenberg is addicted to conscience, and his conscience is rooted in a love for the Jewish people that transcends fidelity to a particular denomination. He believes in dialogue. He believes in speaking to all kinds of Jews—Jewish secularists, Jewish atheists, members of the Jewish Community Center, of the Jewish Federations, and Jews of all religious denominations. But conscience costs. And it costs him a great deal.

In 1987, Greenberg visited England with an idea to parallel his remarkable program of CLAL, which gathered together Jewish rabbis of all denominations to study together. In England, he was told by the Orthodox rabbinic leadership that he could neither speak nor participate with the Reform rabbis, lest he legitimate Reform rabbis and himself become delegitimated.

So Greenberg appealed to the Chief Rabbi of England, Sir Emanuel Jacobovitz, and he was turned down. Greenberg had been invited to speak at the Orthodox Marble Arch Synagogue, and the invitation was summarily rescinded.

When Greenberg first dared to engage in a dialogue between us, among us, an intra-dialogue between Reform and Conservative and Orthodox and Reconstructionists, he was warned not to do so. But more importantly, he was brought up on charges of heresy, in violation of Orthodox discipline, before his rabbinic organization. But the Rabbinic Council of America—for pragmatic, political reasons—decided not to do that, and Greenberg was not formally excommunicated. Too bad, I say. Had he been cast out, he would have been numbered among the greats—Spinoza, Maimonides, Mordecai Kaplan. In my opinion, it is better to be numbered among the excommunicated, than among those who excommunicate.

DISCUSSION 6

ON SPEAKING TO THE NON-JEWISH COMMUNITY

RABBI FEINSTEIN:

We have talked about overcoming divides. Rabbi Kushner, your books sell far beyond the Jewish community. Your reputation goes far beyond the Jewish community. I'm curious to know, on a personal level, what you've learned from your conversations with non-Jews, and on a more general level, what the Jewish people have to teach the world.

RABBI KUSHNER:

What I'm hearing is that a lot of the clichés my generation grew up with are not true. There's a tremendous amount of *ahavat Yisrael* [love for the Jewish people] out there. I was astonished in 1981, and I remain astonished twenty-three years later, at the readiness of American Christians to learn about God from a Conservative rabbi. I would not have believed it. I first became aware of this shortly after my first book was published and I went on a very extensive book tour. And at one point, they sent me to Houston, Texas. I remember landing at Houston

127

International Airport, saying to myself, "*Gevalt,* this is Bible Belt country. What am I doing here? I will consider this a success if they only burn me in effigy and let me leave town alive."

I got on a talk show and all of a sudden, these Baptists started to call in. And a woman said, "Rabbi, thank you for writing a book to remind us that God loves us. He's not punishing us." And a minister called in and said, "Rabbi, thank you so much for that book. Instead of spending two hours talking to a grieving parishioner, I can give her the book, and she'll read it when she's ready for it." I was totally unprepared for that.

The idea that these people recognized the authenticity of the Jewish message—the right of Jews to teach them what God said to us in God's first public utterance—was amazing. I think it's something that we who grew up on stories of pogroms and anti-Semitism were not prepared for.

What do we have to teach others? First, I would teach the wonderful Jewish insight that community precedes theology and that we belong to each other like a family, not only because we believe in the same things. We can believe differently because we have different communities. When my neighbor says to me, "You know, my wife has got to be the most wonderful woman in the world," he is not issuing a statement of fact, but one of love and loyalty. He's not really saying that his wife is the most wonderful woman in the world. He's saying how much he loves his wife. And when my neighbor gets up in the stands of a football game and holds up a sign that says, "John 3:16," which says essentially, "My religion is the only way to heaven," I don't have to argue theology with him. I can say to him, "Yes, I know how important my faith is to my life and I can appreciate how important your faith is to yours." I don't have to challenge what he's saying. Community precedes theology.

Second, we have to teach the world the potential holiness of the ordinary deed, the ordinary life, the ordinary moment. If I had to define Torah in one sentence, it would be the science of taking the ordinary and sanctifying it. I would teach people how to say that, how to do that.

Third, we have a lesson to teach the world about what it means to pray. Jews understand that prayer is not bargaining with God. Prayer is thanking and prayer is studying and prayer is being reminded before prayer is asking. This is how you can avoid saying, "I prayed for something and God didn't give it to me. Was I not worthy or is God mean?"

I was surprised by the readiness of Christians to listen to those messages. One of the miracles of recent American history is the openness of various faith traditions, not simply to meet with each other, but to learn from each other. I know, and I suspect we all know, Jews who have introduced elements of Buddhist meditation into their prayer life. I know Christians who observe a Jewish Sabbath as the day of disengagement from the world as well as going to church on Sundays. I know Buddhists who are fascinated by the Christian notion of a God who enters into our suffering to make us suffer less. We are enriched by this kind of sharing. And I think that it is very much our role to try and lead the way on that.

RABBI SCHULWEIS:
I would add that what is interesting is not just how many millions of people have read Harold Kushner's books,

129

but *who* that readership includes. People from all walks of life, deists and theists, agnostics, atheists, secularists, religionists, those who believe, those who don't believe, and those who make believe, Jews and Christians alike read Rabbi Kushner's books.

How does he manage to write with such a universalistic embracing perspective with a pen that is dipped into the indelible ink of particularity? How is it that he is so accessible? In his modern classic, *When Bad Things Happen to Good People*, he gives it all away. He writes in the opening lines: "This is not an abstract book about God and theology. It does not try to use big words or clever ways of rephrasing questions...." But Harold Kushner's appeal lies not in his accessible style alone. It is in his singular approach to spirituality, to religion and to theology. Rabbi Kushner writes in the mode of what our mutual teacher, Abraham Joshua Heshel, once called "depth theology."

In depth theology you ask, who in the world are you *before* you entered into the synagogue? Who are you *before* you entered into the mosque? Who are you *before* you entered into the church? Who are you, what made you *before* you entered into the ashram?

This is the antecedent of religion and belief, and Harold knows this. His readers don't share a catechism in common. But they share tears in common. He knows that his readers do not share a doctrine in common. But they share fears in common. They share no dogmas in common. But they share hopes in common.

And we can all know this commonality well, too. Just enter into the corridors of the hospital, the hospice, the wedding hall. Harold Kushner, as father, rabbi, and human being, knows the parents' anguish over the sickness of their children, the fright of dying and of death, the cries of the newborn child and the songs of marriage. His books are drawn from a raw material—the birth pangs of all religion. From some existentialist reality, he touches the reader beneath his or her ecclesiastical skin. And he has the genius to translate theological jargon into a common universe of discourse.

For in dealing with a problem of suffering, where others may deal with theodicy, the justification of God in the face of evil, Harold Kushner looks into the eyes of the bereaved, into the eyes of the mourner. He is less interested in defending the omnipotence or the perfection of God than in defending the goodness of God, a goodness that is to be loved and to be acted out by family, friends, and community.

Rabbi Kushner persuades us that God and faith are based not in the search for the cause, but in the response. His theodicy, his *Tziduk Hadin*, is superseded by *nihum aveilim*—the consolation of the mourner. And it is out of comfort and consolation that he builds his theology. Rabbi Kushner is not one to surrender to a forced rationalization of tragedy that will wave the magic wand over the darkness and turn it into light.

ON THE MEANING
OF THE HOLOCAUST

RABBI FEINSTEIN:

This generation has been shaped by two historical events—the Shoah and the birth of the State of Israel. But within a very few years, those who witnessed those events will all be gone. And those two events will be relegated to history. Jewish families will sit down, as they sit down now at Pesach, to tell a story. There was a time when the rabbis of the tradition decided what *Yitziat Mitzraim* [the Exodus from Egypt] meant, and that forms the contents of our Haggadah. What will we decide is the meaning of the Holocaust? What will we teach our children to learn from it? What should we teach our children not to learn from it? What place does it have in the negotiation of our identity in the next generation?

RABBI SCHULWEIS:

I think that it is extremely important to not allow the Holocaust to so eclipse the whole world that all you see and all you hear about it is *b'chol dor vador omdim aleinu l'chaloteinu* [in every generation they rise up to destroy us]. Such an outlook is extremely depressing. According to Martin Gilbert, Ben-Gurion was extremely agitated and very worried during the Eichmann trial because the evidence poured in of the unbelievable cruelty and the isolation of the Jewish people and the hatred toward them. Ben-Gurion asked the Holocaust center, Yad Vashem, to find twenty-four Christians who risked their lives to save Jews during the Holocaust, because he did not want his people to be left with a sense of hopelessness and despair and the belief that the whole world hates us.

One of the most transforming experiences in my life was meeting hundreds of Christians, Poles, and Germans who risked their lives to save Jews in the Holocaust. These encounters lifted my morale. There are remarkable stories from people like Sempo Sugihara and Alexander Roslin and events like the village of Le Chambon or the nation of Bulgaria, or the Italian army, all of whom made extraordinary efforts to save Jews from the Nazis. These stories have to be celebrated and known, because they're true, and yet they're not being remembered.

I remember meeting Harry Cargas, and Father Pawlikowski and the Eckhardts, and realizing, thank God, that we're really not alone. I know that it was a great *novum* in this community when we brought to our synagogue Cardinal Mahoney on two occasions. One occasion was the recognition by the Vatican of the State of Israel, the other was the mea culpa statement of the Church. My *zeyde* would never have believed this. Here was a cardinal, here were priests, here were ministers, here were nuns, people who really had a deep longing to overcome this history of contempt. I think it's possible, I think it's important to include these stories in the history of the Holocaust. And what's more, there's no *b'reirah* [alternative].

RABBI GREENBERG:

I think that the lack of Jewish response to the Holocaust is a classic example of the failure of all three denominations. In our lifetime, and certainly in the last century, two of the greatest events of Jewish history have occurred: a *churban* [destruction] greater than the *churban Bayit Shenee* or *Rishon* [destruction of the First or Second Temple], which were the most influential events in Jewish history up until now, and a redemption, in my judgment, no less and maybe greater than *Yitziat Mitzraim* [the Exodus from Egypt]. If the Rabbis decreed that at every wedding we should break a glass, and if the Rabbis decreed that every house remain unfinished, because of the destruction of the Temple, what's the equivalent symbolism for the Holocaust? I believe that's what we Jews should all be doing. If the Orthodox were truly halachic, they would have done so, and the fact that they haven't calls into question their credentials and turns them into preservationists.

The same applies to the other two denominations. Reform should have been the leader in this, but they resisted. To this day I do not think that there is adequate liturgical recognition of either of the two events. In later editions, the *Siddur Sim Shalom* and the Reform prayer book are better, but they're certainly very far from adequate.

Why isn't there a *megillah* [a scroll, a liturgical scripture] for this? The most seriously attempted modern *megillah* was written by Abba Kovner, who presents himself as a secular Jew. I think the rabbis should be asking themselves these very questions. The Shoah brings out among some Jews a negative theology, and it shakes their belief in God, leading to exaggerated Jewish "anti-goyism." But the negativity is only part of the reality of the Holocaust. The other part is that such events have the power to transform. How can you not be transformed by the Holocaust? How can you go on praying in the same way? The fact that all three denominations went on *davening* after the Shoah the same way as before is deeply shameful. To not argue with God, to not question, to not admit that there are serious problems, is to be in denial. And yet all three major denominations chose not to change their respective prayer books even an inch.

Beyond the Holocaust, what about Israel and Yom Ha-Atzmaut? How about *Hallel*? How about celebrating with a Haggadah? How about a feast? How about celebrating a hundred other ways? *Yitziat Mitzraim* [the Exodus from Egypt] is remembered every single day, three times a day, as well as on Passover and Shabbat. Isn't the creation of the State of Israel an incredible opportunity for creative rabbis who take liturgy seriously to create new prayers?

I would argue that these two events will be, before we're done, at the core of the Jewish religious calendar, at the core of Jewish religious halachic observance in all of the denominations.

RABBI KUSHNER:

I share Rabbi Greenberg's frustration and the frustration of the whole panel on this issue. I would agree that the Shoah and the establishment of Israel were epochal events in our lifetime. But I think it's too soon. It is soon to understand those events in the perspective of history while the people who went through them are still alive.

One of the effective things about religious ritual is that it carries the weight of generations of tradition, of precedent. It's a very hard thing to start a new ritual. Moshe Rabbenu faces this in Deuteronomy, when he speaks to people who were not at Sinai—people whose parents and grandparents were at Sinai, but who weren't there themselves. For them it's a story. And he doesn't know how to talk to them that way. He talks to them as if they have been there themselves because he hasn't figured out, as later generations would figure out, how to create a seder and write a Haggadah and invent rituals.

It's an astonishing thing that in the twentieth century, we invented two new rituals and we added new dates to the Jewish calendar. This has not happened for a long time. What were the two? Bat mitzvah and unveiling. And they work because they responded to human needs.

I think we will do what this panel has said. We will try in our various denominations. We will try various kinds of things, and see what works and what catches on. And we will gain the perspective to understand what is the enduring lesson that we want to have Jews tell each other and tell their children and tell the world.

RABBI ELLENSON:

Harold Schulweis has taught us how important it is not to look at the history of Judaism in the twentieth century as a lachrymose one, despite the temptation to do so. If I were to look at the totality of Jewish history and I were to ask what were the greatest events that marked and formed our people, I would see a series of destructions and comebacks. After the destruction of the First Temple, and the beginning of the *t'futzot* [diaspora], Ezra and the scribes emerged in Babylon, signaling that unlike the destruction at the hands of the Assyrians, our people don't disappear. This is the beginning of the "people of the book." After the destruction of the Second Temple, we have Yochanan ben Zakkai and Yavneh, and our Judaism comes to be a portable religion. We have a halachic Judaism that is able to survive in a shadow kind of way, even as we no longer have the land.

Then there comes the Emancipation, and for the first time to be a Jew is a matter of voluntary identity. The Jewish people are still attempting to respond to that. Our loss of political autonomy is a crisis that we have never been able to adequately address. The denominations are outcomes of that larger transformation, not the causes of it.

After Emancipation, the Shoah and *hakamat Medinat Yisrael* (the establishment of the State of Israel) mark the greatest events in Jewish history. Here I would cite an article by Yitz Greenberg called "Auschwitz, Beginning of the New Era," which I taught in my Jewish thought classes every single year at the Hebrew Union College. In that article, Rabbi Greenberg indicts everybody. He says that the Jews didn't do enough. And he asks what it means to have a Christian ethos of infinite love for persons when, in a culture permeated with Christian teachings, this type of evil could occur? At the same time, enlightenment and secularism prove not to be sufficiently strong to cause people to do the good.

When I contemplate an event like the Shoah, I would add that we Jews lived by two myths. One is what I call the rabbinic myth of the dual Torah, the Written and Oral Law. And then there's a Judaism of destruction and redemption that we lived through in the twentieth century—the Holocaust and the rise of the Jewish state. Sometimes the two coincide. But to some degree, they're completely different forms of Judaism. Our challenge is to try to integrate them. As someone born at the close of the Second World War, my own life, my own way of being in the world cannot be understood outside the context of the State of Israel.

I was entered into the covenant at my *b'rit milah* on November 29, 1947 [the date of the United Nations' vote establishing the State of Israel]. My wife happened to find my bar mitzvah speech a couple of months ago. It was titled "The Thirteenth Year of the State of Israel." My whole life has been spent going back and forth between Israel and the United States. This is not just an individual spiritual quest or journey. To me, what lies at the very heart of Judaism is the love for the Jewish people. And how can people express that love for the Jewish people and know what it is if they don't experience the living reality of Jewish autonomy within a Jewish state? The *Birkat Kohanim* [the Priestly Blessing] is one of my favorite blessings. Before the *kohanim* bless the people, they recite the words, *Baruch ata Adonai Eloheynu melech ha-olam asher kid'shanu bikdushato shel Aharon v'tsivanu l'varech et amo Yisrael b'ahavah* [Blessed is God, Ruler of the Universe, who has sanctified us with the sanctity of Aaron and commanded us to bless God's people Israel *in love*]. We're commanded to love these individual Jewish people, to love them with all of their warts.

At the end of his essay, Rabbi Greenberg says that part of what we learn from the Holocaust is that to be powerless is not necessarily a morally superior stance. What does it mean to live in a world where people do not exercise power? Where you cannot, at the very most basic level, protect your own children? That is a moral requirement.

The State of Israel represents an unprecedented opportunity for the Jewish people to make their mark in the world. We spoke before about being ashamed. I am often ashamed, I'll be frank, of different political policies that the government of the State of Israel follows in given instances. But simultaneously, I thank God every day that we're even in the position to wrestle with these questions. It is easy to stand in a morally superior position when you do not have power, and to fault other people for how power is exercised. It is much harder to face the responsibility that Israel confronts. When we talk about the meaning of the events of the twentieth century, what we truly articulate is what it means to take power seriously, and not to wallow in a lachrymose view of history.

As to whether or not Judaism can say something significant to the world, I believe it can. We have talked about ritual. Although I like ritual and observe a great deal of it myself, part of my problem with the traditional Judaism in which I grew up is that the only thing that seemed to genuinely matter was ritual behavior. Of course rituals matter, but what interests me more than how many times a day I *daven,* or which lines I have or have not added at the right moment in my prayers, is whether or not Judaism has a teaching that not only helps people heal in their individual quest, but indicates how a majority government should treat a minority with dignity and respect. How is it you go about creating peace with a neighbor who may in fact, for good reason, dislike and hate you? And how do you not surrender the quest to achieve justice in those kinds of situations?

The real challenge, it seems to me, is not just creating a liturgy for Yom Ha-Atzmaut or Yom HaShoah [Israeli Independence Day and Holocaust Remembrance Day], but to consider our power in modern times. To be powerless in the world in which we live is immoral in and of itself. But how do you exercise power responsibly? And how can Judaism really speak to the significant parts of people's lives?

One of the most powerful sermons I ever heard was several years ago, when Rabbi Schulweis preached on a book that was incredibly meaningful to me personally, *Tuesdays with Morrie*. This book is about the Brandeis University professor who had amytrophic lateral sclerosis. My own father had died of that disease, and I found the book extremely powerful. Rabbi Schulweis made the point that Morrie, the professor, who was so committed to social justice and social action in the world, did not understand that Judaism itself had anything to teach about this topic. He'd been raised in a Socialist Jewish family and had, as it were, imbibed it, but he couldn't quote one passage in the Gemara that would have allowed him to frame his life in an authentically Jewish context. And Rabbi Schulweis's indictment that day was, "Why have we rabbis not taught our people these texts?" Judaism does have something to say to the larger world. Ritual questions are crucial; they anchor us in the world and give us a sense of community and identity. But in the end, we have to be able to move beyond that to ask more significant questions.

Finally, there is the issue of reconciling modernity and halachah, and overcoming the problem of an overly inward, ritualistically oriented Judaism. The question was asked, "Can you drink Coca-Cola from a can?"

Halachically, this is a serious question about whether or not you have to *tavel* [immerse in a *mikvah*] the vessel out of which you are going to drink. If the Coca-Cola can constitutes a *kli* [vessel], then it would have to be immersed before you drink it. This is a perfectly logical question, the sort of question that people sitting in yeshivot with too much time on their hands think of all the time. But I almost cried when I read it, not because it's not logically an extension of certain types of halachic argumentation, but because if we spent the same amount of time thinking about how we can give people their proper civil liberties, we would be much better off.

David Hartman writes extremely powerfully on this topic, particularly in his book *Israelis and Jewish Tradition*. If Judaism isn't going to be able to speak to these larger issues, then in the end we're not, as Rabbi Kushner just put it, going to have a great deal to say to the world in light of all the principles and teachings that were put forth. And therefore, when we talk about the Shoah and the State of Israel, I turn to Harold Schulweis's and Yitz Greenberg's writings, and I think that those are the real lessons that we have to learn as we move into the twenty-first century.

ON THE VANISHING AMERICAN JEW

RABBI FEINSTEIN:

In 1964, *Look* magazine had a cover story called "The Vanishing American Jew." In the article, a noted sociologist observed that no ethnic group has ever survived past the third generation in America. In 1964, as the third generation of American Jews was being born and raised, this sociologist predicted that within twenty or so years, there would be no American Jewish community left. Here we are, forty years later. *Look* magazine is gone, and we're here. I'd like to understand why. Is there some sort of resurgent force within the Jewish community, and if so, what is it? And what is the resource for the survival, creativity, and growth of this community, as a community?

RABBI KUSHNER:

You know the story about the Israeli man who asks his neighbor, "Are you an optimist or a pessimist about the peace process?" And the neighbor says, "Me? I'm an optimist." So the guy says, "Why do you look so glum?"

And his neighbor answers, "You think it's easy being an optimist?"

I'm an optimist about the Jewish future, and it's *not* easy. I have two grounds for optimism. The one I'm less confident in is a little story that I heard years ago about how one winter the French government set out to eradicate wild foxes who were killing livestock and spreading disease. They set a bounty on the foxes, put out poison, and paid people for every carcass they brought in. In two months, they killed half of the wild foxes in France. The following spring, female foxes had litters twice their usual size.

Ahad Ha-Am, in one of his more speculative essays, talks about the *chefetz hakiyyum*—the will to survive—which is found not only in individuals, but in communities. I think the Jewish community possesses the opposite of a death wish. They have a survival wish, which prompted the Jewish community to bounce back from a period of illiteracy and assimilation, a time of embarrassment at being Jewish, and to become the assertive community that we are today. That's half the answer.

The other half is that what we are offering is something people cannot live without: A guide to making sense of the world. A guide to holding onto yourself when things go badly. A guide to investing your life with meaning. A guide to seeing a human being as more than simply a biological quirk, and as something of infinite value. These are things you can only get from religion.

In the same way that in the 1960s people said the family was obsolete, those who are now saying religion is a crutch will soon learn that religion is a crutch just like food is a crutch for people, who can't nourish themselves with photosynthesis. Religion is so ultimately indispensable that people will wake up, sooner or later, to the fact that they need it.

RABBI SCHULWEIS:

This may shock many of you, but there's wisdom outside of the Jewish community. One of those wise men is William James, who once said, dealing with a question of optimism and pessimism, that he prefers the word "meliorism." It's a highfalutin word, but there it is.

Meliorism is the capacity for improvement, but not the automatic assumption that things are going to be better tomorrow. I learned it, also, when I went to Yeshiva University. Shmuel Mersky, a wonderful teacher, once said, "You have to understand that when you ask questions about optimism or pessimism, you must answer like the *navi,* like the prophet. The prophet always said one word before everything he predicted—*im*—which means "if."

Everything is contingent. If we are a mature community, if we learn to love each other, if we study, if we transmit our knowledge to our children and our children's children, there will be an optimistic end. If we do not, it will not automatically mean survival. We might not survive. Isaiah said, *Edai atem,* "'You are my witnesses, I am God,' says God" (Isaiah 43:12). And then the Rabbis add, "If you are my witnesses, then God is God. But if you are not my witnesses, then God is no longer God."

RABBI FEINSTEIN:

Rabbi Hartman, what do you think is the future of Judaism outside of Israel? Is there a future there? Do you agree with those who argue that Jewish life outside Israel is futile?

Rabbi Hartman:

No. I would never write off any community. It depends on what they do with it. Jews have created a great culture—great lives, great family lives, great schools of learning, great scholars. But today, given the multiple options from which people can choose their identity, it's a different situation than a hundred years ago. Then, Jews were fighting for entry into general society. But now, they're into the opera and the symphony, the arts, museums and hospitals. They've made it among the *goyim*. Jews are in politics, they have power. They're in the administration, they're in Congress, they're in the Senate. They're not a marginalized community.

When today's American Jews send their kids to college, a Hebrew-school education is not enough to counteract what they find there. In colleges, there is an overmoralizing of the Jewish nation—expecting from them who knows what? The kids see the Jews as a moral failure, and they don't want to be part of it. They criticize the Jewish people, but not from inside the *mishpacha* [family]. I often say, "I want to be criticized by my mother, not my mother-in-law." Don't be a mother-in-law who celebrates criticism and enjoys it! To a mother, it hurts. These people, it doesn't hurt them. They celebrate their moral superiority.

I don't see today's great religious intensity as normal. Jews have become *charedi* [ultra-Orthodox] and *baalei t'shuvah* [newly religious] or Lubavitch. But I don't see a healthy, say, "Hartmanian" or "Schulweisian" Judaism surfacing with religious passion in any city in America, by the typical Jew who goes to *shul,* is a member of the board, and contributes to UJA.

146

There isn't any real religious passion there. They're embarrassed by any form of religious enthusiasm.

I don't need the Diaspora to fail in order to confirm my Zionism. I don't need Jews to feel frightened in America to confirm my Zionism. I don't need a failing community there to confirm my legitimacy here. I would want them to be very successful communities. But I don't see it coming. In Israel, there isn't yet a haven of Jewish spirituality. But there is something there you can build on. I still believe that.

ON THE MEANING
OF PLURALISM

RABBI FEINSTEIN:

How do we keep pluralism from melting into relativism, into a sense in which anything goes and there are no standards and no authority for truth?

RABBI SCHULWEIS:

Pluralism embraces with joy the diversity of our old-new people. Pluralism, properly understood, does not give sanction to anarchy, or justification to moral indifference. Pluralism understands the variety of Jewish perspectives, none of which is absolutized as the single truth, or the single conception of God, or the single meaning of revelation. Pluralism is the outlook of modest thinkers, wary of the rigidity of the apodictic certainty that sees the world through one eye. Nor does pluralism proclaim every view as of equal merit.

It is told that in a certain town, one of the disciples of the rabbi warned him that the village atheist was preparing himself with an armory of arguments to challenge the belief of a rabbi. One day, the *apikoros* blew into the rabbi's study, prepared to devastate his faith in God and man. Their eyes met, and the rabbi spoke a single word: *Efshar,* "Perhaps." With that one word, the tension was broken, and the two fell into each other's arms. *Efshar.* Pluralism is not ashamed of terms like "perhaps," "maybe," or "on the other hand." Honest doubt is not the enemy of faith, nor is honest faith the adversary of doubt.

RABBI GREENBERG:

Classically, all religions, not just ours, took a position on truth that I would call "absolutism." In Judaism, this is the position that God has revealed every word of the Torah and that every letter is truth. That absolutism was unlimited and infinite. Anybody who disagreed, therefore, was less valid. Christianity was considered to be a false religion, based on myths that are incredible.

The Jews were not alone in their absolutism, which is also found in Christianity, in which God became flesh only in their religion. Therefore, Judaism is superseded. Therefore, no other religion has this truth.

Absolutism denies and degrades the other religion, but also ends up degrading the person. Because if Judaism is inferior, why are the Jews practicing it?

Absolutism is not morally tenable. It's a *chillul HaShem,* a desecration of God's name. But what's the alternative? It seems that once you no longer have absolute claims, anything goes, because where do you draw the line?

Pluralism simply is the moral and spiritual alternative to absolutism or relativism.

Relativism is deadly. It recognizes no values. According to that view, the SS's evil is just a different style. I may not like it, but I can't condemn it.

Pluralism, by contrast, is the understanding that I have absolute values, like the belief that God was revealed and chose the Jewish people, but I accept limits on that absolute. God's love, in singling out the Jewish people and in revealing to them, does not exhaust God's love.

The verse from the prophet Amos, "God saved the Jews from Egypt," is an expression of love and covenant. But Amos continues: "God also saved the Philistines from Kaftor and God saved Arameans" (Amos 9:7). Isaiah says that the day will come when Israel, Egypt, and Assyria, the two worst enemies of Israel, will all be covenantal people (Isaiah 19:23–25).

So we have a precedent for pluralism. God's love for me does not exhaust God's infinite love. God can love Christians as Christians. God can love Buddhists as Buddhists. God can love and speak to Muslims in Muslim language. If you respect *tzelem Elohim,* the uniqueness of the human being, you believe that.

Therefore, it's entirely possible that Judaism is the true and valid religion, and God has been experienced that way. We disagree with Christianity. We don't believe that God became flesh. But it's not for me to say that God is not speaking in Christianity to Christians. For that matter, you can say that God, in the Christian context, speaks and becomes flesh in Jesus.

In other words, we have to understand our own limits. Christians don't have to deny their belief in Jesus as part of God. They have to accept that even if that's true, it doesn't mean God will not speak again, in a different way, to Jews or to Muslims.

If Jesus denied our religion, he would have been a false messiah. But if Christianity no longer denies our religion, if they're willing to repent and are willing to admit it—then he's not a false messiah.

A false messiah is someone like Shabbetai Tzvi, who claims that "sin will bring you to redemption." A messiah who preaches death over life is a false messiah. But a messiah who teaches, "Love your neighbor as yourself" and "Love God," as the core of the tradition, a messiah who teaches, "You shall help the poor" is not a false messiah.

As a Jew I look at the case of Jesus and I say, "I'm sorry—he didn't make it. He tried to be the Messiah, but the world is still unredeemed. I should be such a failure!" Hundreds of millions of people love and show concern and show justice out of respect to following him. So I consider it a very honorific title to call him a *"failed messiah."*

By the way, I totally failed with this argument. The Orthodox Jews interpreted the argument to mean that I think Jesus was the Messiah, which is a Christian belief, and they're ready to expel me. Meanwhile, the Christians said, "What do you mean *failed*? Failed means you're insulting Jesus." So they rejected it, too.

The truth is, they shouldn't have rejected it when I said "failed." That's how Jesus presents himself in the New Testament. He failed. They put him to death, they killed him, and he did not liberate. That's the point.

All I'm saying is that we don't have to be right. We don't have to win the argument. Accepting limitations is what covenant is all about. God, too, in order to be helpful to humans, had to accept limitations.

RABBI SCHULWEIS:

What concerns me most is that our people don't know that what Rabbi Greenberg is saying now has antecedent roots. He quoted something that I introduced during the *Parashat Zachor*. Instead of reading about the genocidal attitude toward the Amalakites [1 Samuel 15:2–3, 4, traditional haftarah for Parshat Zachor], we added a haftarah from Isaiah. And in that haftarah we read: *Baruch ami Mitzraim, umaseh yadai ashur v'nachlati Yisrael*, "Blessed be Egypt, my people, and Syria, the work of my hands, and Israel, my inheritance" (Isaiah 19:25). Jews said that. The prophets said that.

Secondly, we talked a lot about halachah, and there's a pluralism in halachah. I wish more Jews knew about an Orthodox rabbi by the name of Menachem HaMaeri who lived in the fourteenth century during a time of tremendous persecution. He had to confront the fact that there were many laws based on the Talmud prohibiting traffic with a gentile, laws against greeting gentiles on the holidays, and worse.

Menachem HaMaeri got up and said, "Nonsense. I want you to know that everything that the Talmud speaks about in the past refers to *akum*—to pagans. But we are dealing with *umot hag'durot b'darche datot*—nations that live within the restraints of ethical traditions." That's remarkable. I don't think our people know this. We're not talking about a so-called outsider. We're talking about one of the greatest Talmudists in our history.

To be a Jew is to think big. To be a Jew is to share the covenant with other traditions. To be a Jew is to widen the horizons of our own community, and to become theologically inclusive and remember over and again the heroism of Jewish universalism, which stresses that we are all the children of Adam and Eve and that the God we worship, who freed Jews from the clutches of

Egypt, also brought Philistines out of Caftor and Arameans from Kir.

So what you are doing, Rabbi Greenberg, is carrying a tradition that has been too prematurely buried and repressed. And I want to encourage you. Your heresy is really the deepest fidelity to Judaism that I know of.

We Jews have a lot of blessings, one hundred blessings a day. We'll recite a blessing over wine, over bread, over a rainbow, over the seeing of the ocean for the first time, over the blossoming of trees. But there is also a blessing that we recite over ourselves. And it's a remarkable blessing. When you see a community assembly, you respond, "Blessed is God, who discerns the secrets of each one's heart." For the mind of each is different from the other, just as the face of each is different from the other. This blessing represents the Talmudic celebration of diversity and the gift of diversity, and the blessing of pluralism, and it will be, I am convinced, the unifying thread that binds us together.

DISCUSSION 10

ON COVENANTAL THEOLOGY AND THE SELF-LIMITED GOD

RABBI FEINSTEIN:

Rabbi Greenberg, your covenantal theology represents stages of the self-limitation of God to allow room for the exercise of human will and human intellect as well as human responsibility in the face of evil. So where is God in your life and in your world? For the conventional believer who wants a sense of God's presence in life, what is God's role in life? How do you celebrate God as redeemer of history, present in the triumphs and tragedies of the Jewish people?

RABBI GREENBERG:

When the Rabbis said God is self-limited, they actually meant that God is more present. That's one of the things people misunderstand most in my writings in general. The more God is hidden, the more God is present.

In the biblical period, when God is so present that there are miracles and lightning bolts and floods and so on, God is concentrated in the *Beit Hamikdash* (the Temple of Jerusalem). And if you walk into the Temple and you touch the wrong place, you drop dead, literally. You touch the Holy Ark, it's like high-voltage wire. God is highly concentrated, visible in certain places, and not in other places. So you don't have to be intelligent, you don't have to be understanding in that context, because everything is obvious. That's the biblical experience.

The Rabbis' insight is that God becomes more hidden with time. This means you can have a synagogue not just in Jerusalem. You can have a synagogue anywhere in the world. You can walk into a *shul* without preparation—you don't have to go through a ritual purification. And you won't be struck by lightning if you touch the wrong objects.

But God is present in more places today than in biblical times. That means you can bring a sacrifice not just at the altar in Jerusalem, but by picking your food and serving it in your home with a *b'rachah*, a blessing. So God is more present, more accessible to us today, even if we don't see clear signs of God's presence. Because God is totally hidden, God is present everywhere.

This began in the second era, when Jews first had to discover God for themselves. Without a Temple to rely on, the Rabbis set up *talmud Torah* [the story of Torah]. They knew that people could no longer remain ignorant peasants who came to the Holy Temple in Jerusalem and didn't understand a word of the prayers that went along with their sacrifices. That time had ended, and people needed to be equipped to discover God on their own. And to discover God, they made a *b'rachah* when they ate foods.

Today, I will not see God in the obvious way. But when I see my wife, I see someone I love. I recognize the *tzelem Elohim* of this person, their uniqueness. When you make love to somebody, you recognize their value, their uniqueness, you fall in love with it. You touch it, you feel it, you stroke it, you feel pleasure. You discover the image of God in that moment, and God is present. The Talmud said, long before me, "When a man and woman are worthy, and they make love, God is there."

When you have a sense of reverence for life, when you see a rainbow, when you treat a human being as the image of God and you pay them a decent salary, you experience God. There are a thousand places where God is present, but you have to be trained, you have to be sensitized to recognize that presence. That's the task.

Now you ask me, what is God doing if God is not punishing? Now I disagree with David Hartman in one way. God, I believe, is present in history. Maybe at one time God split the sea. He doesn't do that anymore. Not because God doesn't care, and not because God has disappeared. But because, literally, like a great teacher, God began at the beginning, bringing us in, telling us what to do, guiding us. As we got older, God punished us less and let us grow up.

What is God to us now that we have reached a certain maturity? God is the one who calls me and commands me. But I respond voluntarily. God sets an example. I'm supposed to imitate God's love, God's passion. I imitate God's power and use it for life. God uses power for life. Evil uses power for death.

So I have to choose life and walk in God's path, not just like the often quoted magnificent midrash: "As God is merciful, you be merciful." Rabbi Soloveitchik taught me, "God is powerful; you be powerful." But you have to use your power like God does—for life, not for death; for creation, not for pollution. And that is what God does. Number one, God commands me, God calls me. God escorts me, God sustains me.

It's very important to know someone loves me in my misery. Sometimes I'm a desperate person, but someone loves me. Sometimes I'm an ugly person. Sometimes I do things that I'm ashamed of. God knows these things and still accepts me. God still loves me. That's a tremendously powerful force.

Sometimes you feel lost, cut off, heartbroken. And under those circumstances, God is there sharing that pain. You all know the experience: You try to comfort somebody in shivah, or in sickness, and you have nothing to say. No words will help. But being there, sharing the pain, is tremendously helpful to the person who is suffering.

So my answer is, God is sustaining, God is judging. God wants responsibility, accountability. That was the greatness of modernity. I believe God wanted us to take power. But then along came Freud and Nietzsche, who said, "We'll take even more power if you get God off our back." Just the opposite is true. I know that I'm still accountable and that God will judge me. To me, that is the most powerful form of influence, the most powerful form of presence.

Throughout history, human beings were so sick and so weak that they had to turn to God all the time. They offered worship that came from weakness, worship that came from intimidation and fear. I want my children to love me not because I'm going to help them when they're in trouble, not because they're afraid I'm going to punish them, but because they've reached that level of maturity where they've identified with my values and they want to walk in my footsteps. And that is the love of mature equality and dignity.

It's revolutionary in the sense that we have to develop prayers of the powerful. The prayer of the weak is, "Save me, heal me, God, because I'm very sick and no one can help me." The prayer of the powerful, the prayer of the doctor is, "God, I should use my insight. I should get up early in the morning and not be lazy. I should make a house call, and I should really read this x-ray correctly. I should not overindulge, overmedicate, overcontrol, because I should know I'm a covenantal partner; I have to work with the body, with the person."

There are a thousand ways in which not only is God present, but the human in relation to God acts much more responsibly. This is the dream that Jews have always had, to choose life. That is what the religion is all about. It's about affirming, creating life in every action. There's no neutrality. The next word I use can be a word of life or a word of death. Words of death are words of routine, cant, hypocrisy, cliché, empty words. Words of life are words of truth, of challenge, of growth, of potential. The next act I do can be an act of kindness, an act of love, an act of responsibility. Or an act of irresponsibility.

The ultimate implication is that everywhere you discover life, you discover God. Everywhere you create life, you discover the presence of God. Isaiah said it long before me: "The time will come when—*lo ya'ra'u v'lo yash'chetu*—human beings no longer commit evil, no longer hurt, no longer harm" (Isaiah 2:4). The world will be full of knowledge of God, as the waters fill the sea."

How can you know about a God in a world in which children die of cancer? How can you live in a world of God in which people are cruelly tormenting and selling women into sexual slavery and abusing them?

159

There are a thousand ways this world can't know God. But if you will do God's work, you will discover the image of God. If you will save the image of God, if you will nurture it, then you will know God. And if you will know God, that's the Jewish dream. We have never given it up, and we will never give it up. If there was any time to give it up, it was in my lifetime! And yet we didn't.

One thing I always tell rabbis, when I counsel them, is that no matter what, you have to love the Jewish people. They can be an ugly people, sometimes an awful people, and they will drive you crazy! But loving them is the most important thing in the rabbinate. Because if you don't love them, you're going to hate them. They're impossible. They're going to criticize you, they're going to fall asleep during your sermons, they're going to disagree with you. They're going to make your life miserable. They're going to use up your time.

But if you love them, then it all becomes part of the interchange between us. So I can't stress this enough. That is, it seems to me, the moment we're at now. Where you have to have an inner sense of value, an inner sense of love, an inner sense of privilege, that we were chosen—that we are loved infinitely, that we can play this role of a teacher, or a role model, or a coworker.

I don't have to be the whole picture. I don't have to be the perfect one. That's what pluralism's all about. I remember I struggled in the early years with the idea that the Jewish people are responsible to save the world. I said to myself one day, "We are just 14 million people and we have to lift up this whole earth and make it perfect? I'm going to get a hernia!" Then I realized one day, there are 700 million Christians who are going to help. They are also trying to lift. So I felt relief right there. I've got a better chance. If a billion Muslims would accept that responsibility, and then a billion Hindus, and so on, we'd have a chance.

In the end, if we have the inner courage to recognize that we are not the exclusive religion, that we are not always correct, then we will see that there's enough love and enough appreciation and enough life to go around for everybody. The capacity to create life, the capacity to treasure life, to sustain it, is infinite—because in the end, I believe, we are all sustained by this infinite Source of life. *Melech chafetz b'chaim,* the Ruler who desires life. So, let's choose life.

ON HOPE FOR THE FUTURE

RABBI FEINSTEIN:

As rabbis, as fathers, as leaders of communities, and as private individuals, you've all met tragedy, resistance, difficulty. As a community leader, you've read the demographics and all their sourness and bitterness. I'd like to know where you get hope. And what gives you hope as you lead a Jewish community? Rabbi Hartman, you've lived in Israel a long time, through a great deal of struggle. What keeps you from giving up?

RABBI HARTMAN:

Why do I want stay in Israel? That's a very serious question. I just feel I can't abandon this state. I can't abandon the Jews. It's some visceral solidarity I feel with the Jewish people. I just can't let the secularists kill it, with their strange liberal left mindset. And I can't allow the *charedim*, the right-wing yeshiva Orthodox world to destroy it. I feel totally alienated from the secular left. I don't know what they are talking about! What do they want? For us to be defeated, to be murdered? Can we

163

then feel moral? So we can give a lecture on "The Persecuted Jew—The Oppressed Jew"? They're worried about fighting a just war, and their hope is that it doesn't end up as an unjust war. My concern is that I hope it ends up with as few Israeli soldiers killed as possible! They worry about the morality of power. I worry that we have enough power. We do not celebrate the death of the enemy. Not at all. But we are caught in a dilemma in which the terrorists use the other community as instruments for their own violence. What's the normal response of a healthy nation to that phenomenon?

As for the *charedim*, I have a visceral response to what I think their God is and what they think Judaism is. Certain things are beautiful in their world, but certain things are perverse. It's a ghetto mindset in which you try to live insulated from the world. They are not enriched by culture. Instead, they live in an alternative universe! They worship a different God than I do. In some way, we are members of the same religion, and in a deep way, we're not. I enjoy their love of Torah, but I don't like what they think Torah is. And I enjoy their love for their own people, the charity they give for their own group. It's an in-group morality. Their *hiddur mitzvah* [beautifying the commandment] is a very precious thing. And I enjoy the fact that they're not like the rabbis who are complaining all the time that they have *kehillot* that they can't speak to, they can't demand of, that they can't speak *mitzvah* to them. These people don't have that problem. They just hear the wrong commandments.

Facing our shortcomings should not blind us to the marvelous achievements of the past. We have built a home for all Jews. *Galut* (exile) is no more a defining feature of Jewish history. The picture of the homeless, wandering Jew need not haunt our memory of Jewish history. For this we must be joyful and grateful.

RABBI ELLENSON:

I don't know what it would mean to surrender hope. As Simon Rawidowicz put it in one of my favorite essays, we're an ever-dying people, but the converse is therefore also true. To be ever-dying means that we're always living. I don't know how it is that we can surrender hope. There are elements of darkness that exist in the world, but simultaneously, look at the very teaching that's at the heart of Jewish tradition. Human beings, as flawed and finite as we are, are nevertheless deemed by a transcendent, infinite God to be so valuable that we're deemed worthy of being God's partners in the work of creation. That thought alone gives me, in my darker moments, some hope, as does the history of our people and the ongoing nature of our existence.

RABBI KUSHNER:

One summer, when I set out to get in shape to run the Falmouth Road Race, a mini-marathon on Cape Cod, my daughter bought me a T-shirt, and on the back she had printed a verse from her bat mitzvah haftarah portion: "Those who wait upon God shall renew their strength; they shall mount up with wings as eagles; they shall run, and not be weary; and they shall walk, and not faint" (Isaiah 40:31). I find so remarkable the capacity of people to find their strength replenished, and for me that's the proof of the reality of God. We are able to do seemingly impossible things because when we use up all our strength and all our love and all our faith and hope, some source beyond ourselves replenishes it.

Rabbi Greenberg:

I would like to endorse David Ellenson's comment—that the heart of the religion is hope. There are three things in life: facts, dreams, and faith. The dream we hold is not a fact. Faith is the trust that this will happen. Hope is the dream that is backed by a commitment and by activity to turn it into fact. Sometimes a dream is spoiled when it becomes real. But hope is committed to become a fact. Being Jewish is just that: We have this hope, a dream of a perfect world. But our hope is backed up by our commitment and our lives and our religion and our community and our desire to make it a reality.

After war, birthrates jump enormously all over the world. This is because people respond to death with life. Somehow we're connected to life. God is the infinite Source of life, and we respond to death with increased life.

After our son was killed, both his sisters had children. After his death. And I know that it was an act of love, but it was also their act of life, their response to his death. Because they loved him so much and because they felt his life was so missing, they responded by acting. I look back and wonder what God saw in the Jewish people that after the Shoah we had the greatest outburst of life in our history? It's the greatest heroism in our history. But it's not only Jews who act that way—the whole world acts that way. So it's not my hope or my particular quality. I think that's the amazing human capacity to be so rooted in life as to respond to the enemies of life or the destruction of life with the even greater commitment to life and to love.

BOOKS BY
CONTRIBUTORS

Rabbi David Ellenson

After Emancipation: Jewish Religious Responses to Modernity. New York: Hebrew Union College Press, 2004.

Between Tradition and Culture: The Dialectics of Jewish Religion and Identity in the Modern World. Gainesville: University of South Florida, 1994.

Rabbi Esriel Hildesheimer and the Creation of a Modern Jewish Orthodoxy. Tuscaloosa: University of Alabama Press, 2003.

Tradition in Transition: Orthodoxy, Halakhah and the Boundaries of Modern Jewish Identity. Lanham, MD: University Press of America, 1989.

Rabbi Irving "Yitz" Greenberg

For the Sake of Heaven and Earth: The New Encounter between Judaism and Christianity. Philadelphia: Jewish Publication Society, 2004.

The Jewish Way: Living the Holidays. New York: Touchstone, 1993.

Living in the Image of God: Jewish Teachings to Perfect the World, Conversations with Rabbi Irving Greenberg with Shalom Freedman. Northvale, NJ: Jason Aronson, 1998.

Rabbi David Hartman

A Heart of Many Rooms: Celebrating the Many Voices within Judaism. Woodstock, VT: Jewish Lights, 1999.

Israelis and the Jewish Tradition : An Ancient People Debating Its Future. The Terry Lectures Series. New Haven, CT: Yale University Press, 2000.

A Living Covenant: The Innovative Spirit in Traditional Judaism. Woodstock, VT: Jewish Lights, 1998.

Love and Terror in the God Encounter: The Theological Legacy of Rabbi Joseph B. Soloveitchik. Woodstock, VT: Jewish Lights, 2004.

Maimonides: Torah and Philosophic Quest. Philadelphia: Jewish Publication Society, 1976.

Rabbi Harold Kushner

How Good Do We Have to Be? A New Understanding of Guilt and Forgiveness. New York: Back Bay Books, 1997.

Living a Life That Matters: Resolving the Conflict between Conscience and Success. New York: Anchor, 2002.

The Lord Is My Shepherd. New York: Anchor, 2004.

Overcoming Life's Disappointments. New York: Knopf, 2006.

To Life! The Celebration of Jewish Being and Thinking. New York: Warner Books, 1994.

When All You've Ever Wanted Isn't Enough: The Search for a Life That Matters. New York: Fireside, 2002.

When Bad Things Happen to Good People. New York: Anchor, 2004.

When Children Ask about God: A Guide for Parents Who Don't Always Have All the Answers. New York: Schocken, 1995.

Who Needs God? New York: Fireside, 2002.

Rabbi Harold M. Schulweis

Approaches to the Philosophy of Religion. With Daniel J. Bronstein. New York: Prentice Hall, 1954.

Evil and the Morality of God. Hoboken, NJ: KTAV, 1984.

Finding Each Other in Judaism: Meditations on the Rites of Passages from Birth to Immortality. New York: URJ Press, 2001.

For Those Who Can't Believe: Overcoming the Obstacles to Faith. New York: Harper Perennial, 1995.

In God's Mirror. Hoboken, NJ: KTAV, 1990.

Passages in Poetry. Encino, CA: Valley Beth Shalom, 1990l.

When You Lie Down and When You Rise Up. Encino, CA: Valley Beth Shalom, 2001.

Bar/Bat Mitzvah

The JGirl's Guide: The Young Jewish Woman's Handbook for Coming of Age
By Penina Adelman, Ali Feldman, and Shulamit Reinharz
An inspirational, interactive guidebook designed to help pre-teen Jewish girls address the spiritual, educational, and psychological issues surrounding coming of age in today's society. 6 x 9, 240 pp, Quality PB, 978-1-58023-215-9 **$14.99**
Also Available: **The JGirl's Teacher's and Parent's Guide**
8½ x 11, 56 pp, PB, 978-1-58023-225-8 **$8.99**

Bar/Bat Mitzvah Basics: A Practical Family Guide to Coming of Age Together
Edited by Cantor Helen Leneman 6 x 9, 240 pp, Quality PB, 978-1-58023-151-0 **$18.95**

The Bar/Bat Mitzvah Memory Book, 2nd Edition: An Album for Treasuring the
Spiritual Celebration *By Rabbi Jeffrey K. Salkin and Nina Salkin*
8 x 10, 48 pp, Deluxe HC, 2-color text, ribbon marker, 978-1-58023-263-0 **$19.99**

For Kids—Putting God on Your Guest List: How to Claim the Spiritual Meaning
of Your Bar or Bat Mitzvah *By Rabbi Jeffrey K. Salkin*
6 x 9, 144 pp, Quality PB, 978-1-58023-015-5 **$14.99** *For ages 11–13*

Putting God on the Guest List, 3rd Edition: How to Reclaim the Spiritual
Meaning of Your Child's Bar or Bat Mitzvah *By Rabbi Jeffrey K. Salkin*
6 x 9, 224 pp, Quality PB, 978-1-58023-222-7 **$16.99**; HC, 978-1-58023-260-9 **$24.99**
Also Available: **Putting God on the Guest List Teacher's Guide**
8½ x 11, 48 pp, PB, 978-1-58023-226-5 **$8.99**

Tough Questions Jews Ask: A Young Adult's Guide to Building a Jewish Life
By Rabbi Edward Feinstein 6 x 9, 160 pp, Quality PB, 978-1-58023-139-8 **$14.99** *For ages 12 & up*
Also Available: **Tough Questions Jews Ask Teacher's Guide**
8½ x 11, 72 pp, PB, 978-1-58023-187-9 **$8.95**

Bible Study/Midrash

Abraham's Bind & Other Bible Tales of Trickery, Folly, Mercy and Love *By Michael J. Caduto*
Re-imagines many biblical characters, retelling their stories and highlighting their foibles and strengths, their struggles and joys. Readers will learn that God has a way of working for them and through them, even today.
6 x 9, 224 pp, HC, 978-1-59473-186-0 **$19.99** *(A SkyLight Paths book)*

Ancient Secrets: Using the Stories of the Bible to Improve Our Everyday Lives
By Rabbi Levi Meier, PhD 5½ x 8½, 288 pp, Quality PB, 978-1-58023-064-3 **$16.95**

The Genesis of Leadership: What the Bible Teaches Us about Vision,
Values and Leading Change *By Rabbi Nathan Laufer; Foreword by Senator Joseph I. Lieberman*
Unlike other books on leadership, this one is rooted in the stories of the Bible, and teaches the values that the Bible believes are prerequisites for true leadership.
6 x 9, 288 pp, HC, 978-1-58023-241-8 **$24.99**

Hineini in Our Lives: Learning How to Respond to Others through 14 Biblical Texts and
Personal Stories *By Norman J. Cohen* 6 x 9, 240 pp, Quality PB, 978-1-58023-274-6 **$16.99**

Moses and the Journey to Leadership: Timeless Lessons of Effective Management from
the Bible and Today's Leaders *By Dr. Norman J. Cohen* 6 x 9, 250 pp, HC, 978-1-58023-227-2 **$21.99**

Self, Struggle & Change: Family Conflict Stories in Genesis and Their Healing Insights for
Our Lives *By Norman J. Cohen* 6 x 9, 224 pp, Quality PB, 978-1-879045-66-8 **$18.99**

The Triumph of Eve & Other Subversive Bible Tales *By Matt Biers-Ariel*
5½ x 8½, 192 pp, Quality PB, 978-1-59473-176-1 **$14.99**; HC, 978-1-59473-040-5 **$19.99**
(A SkyLight Paths book)

Voices from Genesis: Guiding Us through the Stages of Life *By Norman J. Cohen*
6 x 9, 192 pp, Quality PB, 978-1-58023-118-3 **$16.95**

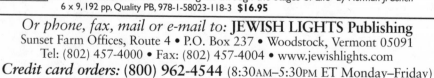

Or phone, fax, mail or e-mail to: **JEWISH LIGHTS Publishing**
Sunset Farm Offices, Route 4 • P.O. Box 237 • Woodstock, Vermont 05091
Tel: (802) 457-4000 • Fax: (802) 457-4004 • www.jewishlights.com
Credit card orders: **(800) 962-4544** (8:30AM–5:30PM ET Monday–Friday)
Generous discounts on quantity orders. SATISFACTION GUARANTEED. Prices subject to change.

Inspiration

God's To-Do List: 103 Ways to Be an Angel and Do God's Work on Earth
By Dr. Ron Wolfson 6 x 9, 150 pp, Quality PB, 978-1-58023-301-9 **$15.99**

God in All Moments: Mystical & Practical Spiritual Wisdom from Hasidic Masters
Edited and translated by Or N. Rose with Ebn D. Leader
5½ x 8½, 192 pp, Quality PB, 978-1-58023-186-2 **$16.95**

Our Dance with God: Finding Prayer, Perspective and Meaning in the Stories of Our
Lives *By Karyn D. Kedar* 6 x 9, 176 pp, Quality PB, 978-1-58023-202-9 **$16.99**

Also Available: **The Dance of the Dolphin** (HC edition of *Our Dance with God*)
6 x 9, 176 pp, HC, 978-1-58023-154-1 **$19.95**

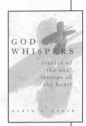

The Empty Chair: Finding Hope and Joy—Timeless Wisdom from a Hasidic Master,
Rebbe Nachman of Breslov *Adapted by Moshe Mykoff and the Breslov Research Institute*
4 x 6, 128 pp, 2-color text, Deluxe PB w/flaps, 978-1-879045-67-5 **$9.95**

The Gentle Weapon: Prayers for Everyday and Not-So-Everyday Moments—
Timeless Wisdom from the Teachings of the Hasidic Master, Rebbe Nachman of Breslov
Adapted by Moshe Mykoff and S. C. Mizrahi, together with the Breslov Research Institute
4 x 6, 144 pp, 2-color text, Deluxe PB w/flaps, 978-1-58023-022-3 **$9.99**

God Whispers: Stories of the Soul, Lessons of the Heart *By Karyn D. Kedar*
6 x 9, 176 pp, Quality PB, 978-1-58023-088-9 **$15.95**

An Orphan in History: One Man's Triumphant Search for His Jewish Roots
By Paul Cowan; Afterword by Rachel Cowan. 6 x 9, 288 pp, Quality PB, 978-1-58023-135-0 **$16.95**

Restful Reflections: Nighttime Inspiration to Calm the Soul, Based on Jewish Wisdom
By Rabbi Kerry M. Olitzky & Rabbi Lori Forman 4½ x 6½, 448 pp, Quality PB, 978-1-58023-091-9 **$15.95**

Sacred Intentions: Daily Inspiration to Strengthen the Spirit, Based on Jewish Wisdom
By Rabbi Kerry M. Olitzky and Rabbi Lori Forman 4½ x 6½, 448 pp, Quality PB, 978-1-58023-061-2 **$15.95**

Kabbalah/Mysticism/Enneagram

Awakening to Kabbalah: The Guiding Light of Spiritual Fulfillment
By Rav Michael Laitman, PhD 6 x 9, 192 pp, HC, 978-1-58023-264-7 **$21.99**

Seek My Face: A Jewish Mystical Theology *By Arthur Green*
6 x 9, 304 pp, Quality PB, 978-1-58023-130-5 **$19.95**

Zohar: Annotated & Explained
Translation and annotation by Daniel C. Matt; Foreword by Andrew Harvey
5½ x 8½, 176 pp, Quality PB, 978-1-893361-51-5 **$15.99** *(A SkyLight Paths book)*

Cast in God's Image: Discover Your Personality Type Using the Enneagram and Kabbalah
By Rabbi Howard A. Addison
7 x 9, 176 pp, Quality PB, Layflat binding, 20+ journaling exercises, 978-1-58023-124-4 **$16.95**

Ehyeh: A Kabbalah for Tomorrow
By Arthur Green 6 x 9, 224 pp, Quality PB, 978-1-58023-213-5 **$16.99**

The Enneagram and Kabbalah, 2nd Edition: Reading Your Soul
By Rabbi Howard A. Addison 6 x 9, 192 pp, Quality PB, 978-1-58023-229-6 **$16.99**

Finding Joy: A Practical Spiritual Guide to Happiness *By Dannel I. Schwartz with Mark Hass*
6 x 9, 192 pp, Quality PB, 978-1-58023-009-4 **$14.95**

The Flame of the Heart: Prayers of a Chasidic Mystic *By Reb Noson of Breslov. Translated by
David Sears with the Breslov Research Institute* 5 x 7¼, 160 pp, Quality PB, 978-1-58023-246-3 **$15.99**

The Gift of Kabbalah: Discovering the Secrets of Heaven, Renewing Your Life on Earth
By Tamar Frankiel, PhD 6 x 9, 256 pp, Quality PB, 978-1-58023-141-1 **$16.95;**
HC, 978-1-58023-108-4 **$21.95**

Kabbalah: A Brief Introduction for Christians
By Tamar Frankiel, PhD 5½ x 8½, 208 pp, Quality PB, 978-1-58023-303-3 **$16.99**

The Lost Princess and Other Kabbalistic Tales of Rebbe Nachman of Breslov
The Seven Beggars and Other Kabbalistic Tales of Rebbe Nachman of Breslov
Translated by Rabbi Aryeh Kaplan; Preface by Rabbi Chaim Kramer
Lost Princess: 6 x 9, 400 pp, Quality PB, 978-1-58023-217-3 **$18.99**
Seven Beggars: 6 x 9, 192 pp, Quality PB, 978-1-58023-250-0 **$16.99**

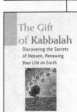

See also *The Way Into Jewish Mystical Tradition* in Spirituality / The Way Into... Series

Holidays/Holy Days

Rosh Hashanah Readings: Inspiration, Information and Contemplation
Yom Kippur Readings: Inspiration, Information and Contemplation
Edited by Rabbi Dov Peretz Elkins with Section Introductions from Arthur Green's These Are the Words
An extraordinary collection of readings, prayers and insights that enable the modern worshiper to enter into the spirit of the High Holy Days in a personal and powerful way, permitting the meaning of the Jewish New Year to enter the heart.
RHR: 6 x 9, 400 pp, HC, 978-1-58023-239-5 **$24.99**
YKR: 6 x 9, 368 pp, HC, 978-1-58023-271-5 **$24.99**

Jewish Holidays: A Brief Introduction for Christians
By Rabbi Kerry M. Olitzky and Rabbi Daniel Judson
5½ x 8½, 144 pp, Quality PB, 978-1-58023-302-6 **$16.99**

Leading the Passover Journey: The Seder's Meaning Revealed, the Haggadah's Story Retold *By Rabbi Nathan Laufer*
Uncovers the hidden meaning of the Seder's rituals and customs.
6 x 9, 224 pp, HC, 978-1-58023-211-1 **$24.99**

Reclaiming Judaism as a Spiritual Practice: Holy Days and Shabbat
By Rabbi Goldie Milgram
7 x 9, 272 pp, Quality PB, 978-1-58023-205-0 **$19.99**

7th Heaven: Celebrating Shabbat with Rebbe Nachman of Breslov
By Moshe Mykoff with the Breslov Research Institute
5⅛ x 8¼, 224 pp, Deluxe PB w/flaps, 978-1-58023-175-6 **$18.95**

The Women's Passover Companion: Women's Reflections on the Festival of Freedom *Edited by Rabbi Sharon Cohen Anisfeld, Tara Mohr, and Catherine Spector*
Groundbreaking. A provocative conversation about women's relationships to Passover as well as the roots and meanings of women's seders.
6 x 9, 352 pp, Quality PB, 978-1-58023-231-9 **$19.99**

The Women's Seder Sourcebook: Rituals & Readings for Use at the Passover Seder *Edited by Rabbi Sharon Cohen Anisfeld, Tara Mohr, and Catherine Spector*
Gathers the voices of more than one hundred women in readings, personal and creative reflections, commentaries, blessings, and ritual suggestions that can be incorporated into your Passover celebration.
6 x 9, 384 pp, Quality PB, 978-1-58023-232-6 **$19.99**

Creating Lively Passover Seders: A Sourcebook of Engaging Tales, Texts & Activities
By David Arnow, PhD 7 x 9, 416 pp, Quality PB, 978-1-58023-184-8 **$24.99**

Hanukkah, 2nd Edition: The Family Guide to Spiritual Celebration
By Dr. Ron Wolfson. Edited by Joel Lurie Grishaver.
7 x 9, 240 pp, illus., Quality PB, 978-1-58023-122-0 **$18.95**

The Jewish Family Fun Book: Holiday Projects, Everyday Activities, and Travel Ideas
with Jewish Themes *By Danielle Dardashti and Roni Sarig. Illus. by Avi Katz.*
6 x 9, 288 pp, 70+ b/w illus. & diagrams, Quality PB, 978-1-58023-171-8 **$18.95**

The Jewish Gardening Cookbook: Growing Plants & Cooking for Holidays
& Festivals *By Michael Brown* 6 x 9, 224 pp, 30+ b/w illus., Quality PB, 978-1-58023-116-9 **$16.95**

The Jewish Lights Book of Fun Classroom Activities: Simple and Seasonal
Projects for Teachers and Students *By Danielle Dardashti and Roni Sarig*
6 x 9, 240 pp, Quality PB, 978-1-58023-206-7 **$19.99**

Passover, 2nd Edition: The Family Guide to Spiritual Celebration
By Dr. Ron Wolfson with Joel Lurie Grishaver 7 x 9, 352 pp, Quality PB, 978-1-58023-174-9 **$19.95**

Shabbat, 2nd Edition: The Family Guide to Preparing for and Celebrating the Sabbath
By Dr. Ron Wolfson 7 x 9, 320 pp, illus., Quality PB, 978-1-58023-164-0 **$19.99**

Sharing Blessings: Children's Stories for Exploring the Spirit of the Jewish Holidays
By Rahel Musleah and Rabbi Michael Klayman
8½ x 11, 64 pp, Full-color illus., HC, 978-1-879045-71-2 **$18.95** *For ages 6 & up*

Life Cycle
Marriage / Parenting / Family / Aging

Jewish Fathers: A Legacy of Love
Photographs by Lloyd Wolf. Essays by Paula Wolfson. Foreword by Rabbi Harold Kushner.
Honors the role of contemporary Jewish fathers in America. Each father tells in his own words what it means to be a parent and Jewish, and what he learned from his own father. Insightful photos.
10¾ x 9⅜, 144 pp with 100+ duotone photos, HC, 978-1-58023-204-3 **$30.00**

The New Jewish Baby Album: Creating and Celebrating the Beginning of a Spiritual Life—A Jewish Lights Companion
By the Editors at Jewish Lights. Foreword by Anita Diamant. Preface by Rabbi Sandy Eisenberg Sasso.
A spiritual keepsake that will be treasured for generations. More than just a memory book, *shows you how—and why it's important*—to create a Jewish home and a Jewish life. 8 x 10, 64 pp, Deluxe Padded HC, Full-color illus., 978-1-58023-138-1 **$19.95**

The Jewish Pregnancy Book: A Resource for the Soul, Body & Mind during Pregnancy, Birth & the First Three Months
By Sandy Falk, MD, and Rabbi Daniel Judson, with Steven A. Rapp
Includes medical information, prayers and rituals for each stage of pregnancy, from a liberal Jewish perspective. 7 x 10, 208 pp, Quality PB, b/w photos, 978-1-58023-178-7 **$16.95**

Celebrating Your New Jewish Daughter: Creating Jewish Ways to Welcome Baby Girls into the Covenant—New and Traditional Ceremonies *By Debra Nussbaum Cohen; Foreword by Rabbi Sandy Eisenberg Sasso* 6 x 9, 272 pp, Quality PB, 978-1-58023-090-2 **$18.95**

The New Jewish Baby Book, 2nd Edition: Names, Ceremonies & Customs—A Guide for Today's Families *By Anita Diamant* 6 x 9, 336 pp, Quality PB, 978-1-58023-251-7 **$19.99**

Parenting As a Spiritual Journey: Deepening Ordinary and Extraordinary Events into Sacred Occasions *By Rabbi Nancy Fuchs-Kreimer*
6 x 9, 224 pp, Quality PB, 978-1-58023-016-2 **$16.95**

Parenting Jewish Teens: A Guide for the Perplexed
By Joanne Doades 6 x 9, 200 pp, Quality PB, 978-1-58023-305-7 **$16.99**

Judaism for Two: A Spiritual Guide for Strengthening and Celebrating Your Loving Relationship *By Rabbi Nancy Fuchs-Kreimer and Rabbi Nancy H. Wiener; Foreword by Rabbi Elliot N. Dorff* Addresses the ways Jewish teachings can enhance and strengthen committed relationships. 6 x 9, 224 pp, Quality PB, 978-1-58023-254-8 **$16.99**

Embracing the Covenant: Converts to Judaism Talk About Why & How
By Rabbi Allan Berkowitz and Patti Moskovitz 6 x 9, 192 pp, Quality PB, 978-1-879045-50-7 **$16.95**

The Guide to Jewish Interfaith Family Life: An InterfaithFamily.com Handbook
Edited by Ronnie Friedland and Edmund Case 6 x 9, 384 pp, Quality PB, 978-1-58023-153-4 **$18.95**

Introducing My Faith and My Community
The Jewish Outreach Institute Guide for the Christian in a Jewish Interfaith Relationship
By Rabbi Kerry M. Olitzky 6 x 9, 176 pp, Quality PB, 978-1-58023-192-3 **$16.99**

Making a Successful Jewish Interfaith Marriage: The Jewish Outreach Institute Guide to Opportunities, Challenges and Resources *By Rabbi Kerry M. Olitzky with Joan Peterson Littman*
6 x 9, 176 pp, Quality PB, 978-1-58023-170-1 **$16.95**

The Creative Jewish Wedding Book: A Hands-On Guide to New & Old Traditions, Ceremonies & Celebrations *By Gabrielle Kaplan-Mayer*
9 x 9, 288 pp, b/w photos, Quality PB, 978-1-58023-194-7 **$19.99**

Divorce Is a Mitzvah: A Practical Guide to Finding Wholeness and Holiness When Your Marriage Dies *By Rabbi Perry Netter; Afterword by Rabbi Laura Geller.*
6 x 9, 224 pp, Quality PB, 978-1-58023-172-5 **$16.95**

A Heart of Wisdom: Making the Jewish Journey from Midlife through the Elder Years
Edited by Susan Berrin; Foreword by Harold Kushner
6 x 9, 384 pp, Quality PB, 978-1-58023-051-3 **$18.95**

So That Your Values Live On: Ethical Wills and How to Prepare Them
Edited by Jack Riemer and Nathaniel Stampfer
6 x 9, 272 pp, Quality PB, 978-1-879045-34-7 **$18.99**

Spirituality

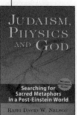

The Adventures of Rabbi Harvey: A Graphic Novel of Jewish Wisdom and Wit in the Wild West *By Steve Sheinkin*
Jewish and American folktales combine in this witty and original graphic novel collection. Creatively retold and set on the western frontier of the 1870s.
6 x 9, 144 pp, Full-color illus., Quality PB, 978-1-58023-310-1 **$16.99**
Also Available: **The Adventures of Rabbi Harvey Teacher's Guide**
8½ x 11, 32 pp, PB, 978-1-58023-326-2 **$8.99**

Ethics of the Sages: *Pirke Avot*—Annotated & Explained
Translation and Annotation by Rabbi Rami Shapiro
5½ x 8½, 192 pp, Quality PB, 978-1-59473-207-2 **$16.99** *(A SkyLight Paths book)*

A Book of Life: Embracing Judaism as a Spiritual Practice
By Michael Strassfeld 6 x 9, 528 pp, Quality PB, 978-1-58023-247-0 **$19.99**

Meaning and Mitzvah: Daily Practices for Reclaiming Judaism through Prayer, God, Torah, Hebrew, Mitzvot and Peoplehood *By Rabbi Goldie Milgram*
7 x 9, 336 pp, Quality PB, 978-1-58023-256-2 **$19.99**

The Soul of the Story: Meetings with Remarkable People
By Rabbi David Zeller 6 x 9, 288 pp, HC, 978-1-58023-272-2 **$21.99**

Aleph-Bet Yoga: Embodying the Hebrew Letters for Physical and Spiritual Well-Being
By Steven A. Rapp. Foreword by Tamar Frankiel, PhD and Judy Greenfeld. Preface by Hart Lazer.
7 x 10, 128 pp, b/w photos, Quality PB, Layflat binding, 978-1-58023-162-6 **$16.95**

Entering the Temple of Dreams: Jewish Prayers, Movements, and Meditations for the End of the Day *By Tamar Frankiel, PhD, and Judy Greenfeld*
7 x 10, 192 pp, illus., Quality PB, 978-1-58023-079-7 **$16.95**

Does the Soul Survive? A Jewish Journey to Belief in Afterlife, Past Lives & Living with Purpose *By Rabbi Elie Kaplan Spitz; Foreword by Brian L. Weiss, MD*
6 x 9, 288 pp, Quality PB, 978-1-58023-165-7 **$16.99**

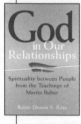

First Steps to a New Jewish Spirit: Reb Zalman's Guide to Recapturing the Intimacy & Ecstasy in Your Relationship with God *By Rabbi Zalman M. Schachter-Shalomi with Donald Gropman* 6 x 9, 144 pp, Quality PB, 978-1-58023-182-4 **$16.95**

God in Our Relationships: Spirituality between People from the Teachings of Martin Buber *By Rabbi Dennis S. Ross* 5½ x 8½, 160 pp, Quality PB, 978-1-58023-147-3 **$16.95**

Judaism, Physics and God: Searching for Sacred Metaphors in a Post-Einstein World
By Rabbi David W. Nelson 6 x 9, 368 pp, Quality PB, inc. reader's discussion guide, 978-1-58023-306-4 **$18.99**;
HC, 352 pp, 978-1-58023-252-4 **$24.99**

The Jewish Lights Spirituality Handbook: A Guide to Understanding, Exploring & Living a Spiritual Life *Edited by Stuart M. Matlins*
What exactly is "Jewish" about spirituality? How do I make it a part of my life? Fifty of today's foremost spiritual leaders share their ideas and experience with us.
6 x 9, 456 pp, Quality PB, 978-1-58023-093-3 **$19.99**

Bringing the Psalms to Life: How to Understand and Use the Book of Psalms
By Daniel F. Polish 6 x 9, 208 pp, Quality PB, 978-1-58023-157-2 **$16.95**;
HC, 978-1-58023-077-3 **$21.95**

God & the Big Bang: Discovering Harmony between Science & Spirituality
By Daniel C. Matt 6 x 9, 216 pp, Quality PB, 978-1-879045-89-7 **$16.99**

Minding the Temple of the Soul: Balancing Body, Mind, and Spirit through Traditional Jewish Prayer, Movement, and Meditation *By Tamar Frankiel, PhD, and Judy Greenfeld*
7 x 10, 184 pp, illus., Quality PB, 978-1-879045-64-4 **$16.95**
Audiotape of the Blessings and Meditations: 60 min. **$9.95**
Videotape of the Movements and Meditations: 46 min. **$20.00**

One God Clapping: The Spiritual Path of a Zen Rabbi *By Alan Lew with Sherril Jaffe*
5½ x 8½, 336 pp, Quality PB, 978-1-58023-115-2 **$16.95**

There Is No Messiah ... and You're It: The Stunning Transformation of Judaism's Most Provocative Idea *By Rabbi Robert N. Levine, DD*
6 x 9, 192 pp, Quality PB, 978-1-58023-255-5 **$16.99**

These Are the Words: A Vocabulary of Jewish Spiritual Life
By Arthur Green 6 x 9, 304 pp, Quality PB, 978-1-58023-107-7 **$18.95**

Spirituality/Lawrence Kushner

Filling Words with Light: Hasidic and Mystical Reflections on Jewish Prayer
By Lawrence Kushner and Nehemia Polen
5½ x 8½, 176 pp, HC, 978-1-58023-216-6 **$21.99**

The Book of Letters: A Mystical Hebrew Alphabet
Popular HC Edition, 6 x 9, 80 pp, 2-color text, 978-1-879045-00-2 **$24.95**
Collector's Limited Edition, 9 x 12, 80 pp, gold foil embossed pages, w/limited edition silkscreened
print, 978-1-879045-04-0 **$349.00**

The Book of Miracles: A Young Person's Guide to Jewish Spiritual Awareness
6 x 9, 96 pp, 2-color illus., HC, 978-1-879045-78-1 **$16.95** *For ages 9 and up*

The Book of Words: Talking Spiritual Life, Living Spiritual Talk
6 x 9, 160 pp, Quality PB, 978-1-58023-020-9 **$16.95**

Eyes Remade for Wonder: A Lawrence Kushner Reader *Introduction by Thomas Moore*
6 x 9, 240 pp, Quality PB, 978-1-58023-042-1 **$18.95**

God Was in This Place & I, i Did Not Know: Finding Self, Spirituality and Ultimate
Meaning 6 x 9, 192 pp, Quality PB, 978-1-879045-33-0 **$16.95**

Honey from the Rock: An Introduction to Jewish Mysticism
6 x 9, 176 pp, Quality PB, 978-1-58023-073-5 **$16.95**

Invisible Lines of Connection: Sacred Stories of the Ordinary
5½ x 8½, 160 pp, Quality PB, 978-1-879045-98-9 **$15.95**

Jewish Spirituality—A Brief Introduction for Christians
5½ x 8½, 112 pp, Quality PB, 978-1-58023-150-3 **$12.95**

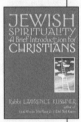

The River of Light: Jewish Mystical Awareness
6 x 9, 192 pp, Quality PB, 978-1-58023-096-4 **$16.95**

The Way Into Jewish Mystical Tradition
6 x 9, 224 pp, Quality PB, 978-1-58023-200-5 **$18.99**; HC, 978-1-58023-029-2 **$21.95**

Spirituality/Prayer

Pray Tell: A Hadassah Guide to Jewish Prayer
By Rabbi Jules Harlow, with contributions from many others
8½ x 11, 400 pp, Quality PB, 978-1-58023-163-3 **$29.95**

Witnesses to the One: The Spiritual History of the *Sh'ma* *By Rabbi Joseph B. Meszler;*
Foreword by Rabbi Elyse Goldstein 6 x 9, 176 pp, HC, 978-1-58023-309-5 **$19.99**

My People's Prayer Book Series

Traditional Prayers, Modern Commentaries *Edited by Rabbi Lawrence A. Hoffman*
Provides diverse and exciting commentary to the traditional liturgy, helping modern
men and women find new wisdom in Jewish prayer, and bring liturgy into their lives.
Each book includes Hebrew text, modern translation, and commentaries from all
perspectives of the Jewish world.
Vol. 1—The *Sh'ma* and Its Blessings
  7 x 10, 168 pp, HC, 978-1-879045-79-8 **$24.99**
Vol. 2—The *Amidah*
  7 x 10, 240 pp, HC, 978-1-879045-80-4 **$24.95**
Vol. 3—*P'sukei D'zimrah* (Morning Psalms)
  7 x 10, 240 pp, HC, 978-1-879045-81-1 **$24.95**
Vol. 4—*Seder K'riat Hatorah* (The Torah Service)
  7 x 10, 264 pp, HC, 978-1-879045-82-8 **$23.95**
Vol. 5—*Birkhot Hashachar* (Morning Blessings)
  7 x 10, 240 pp, HC, 978-1-879045-83-5 **$24.95**
Vol. 6—*Tachanun* and Concluding Prayers
  7 x 10, 240 pp, HC, 978-1-879045-84-2 **$24.95**
Vol. 7—Shabbat at Home
  7 x 10, 240 pp, HC, 978-1-879045-85-9 **$24.95**
Vol. 8—*Kabbalat Shabbat* (Welcoming Shabbat in the Synagogue)
  7 x 10, 240 pp, HC, 978-1-58023-121-3 **$24.99**
Vol. 9—Welcoming the Night: *Minchah* and *Ma'ariv* (Afternoon and
  Evening Prayer) 7 x 10, 272 pp, HC, 978-1-58023-262-3 **$24.99**
Vol. 10—Shabbat Morning: *Shacharit* and *Musaf* (Morning and Additional
  Services) 7 x 10, 240 pp, HC, 978-1-58023-240-1 **$24.99**

Theology/Philosophy/The Way Into... Series

The Way Into... series offers an accessible and highly usable "guided tour" of the Jewish faith, people, history and beliefs—in total, an introduction to Judaism that will enable you to understand and interact with the sacred texts of the Jewish tradition. Each volume is written by a leading contemporary scholar and teacher, and explores one key aspect of Judaism. *The Way Into...* series enables all readers to achieve a real sense of Jewish cultural literacy through guided study.

The Way Into Encountering God in Judaism
By Neil Gillman
For everyone who wants to understand how Jews have encountered God throughout history and today.
6 x 9, 240 pp, Quality PB, 978-1-58023-199-2 **$18.99**; HC, 978-1-58023-025-4 **$21.95**
Also Available: **The Jewish Approach to God:** A Brief Introduction for Christians
By Neil Gillman
5½ x 8½, 192 pp, Quality PB, 978-1-58023-190-9 **$16.95**

The Way Into Jewish Mystical Tradition
By Lawrence Kushner
Allows readers to interact directly with the sacred mystical text of the Jewish tradition. An accessible introduction to the concepts of Jewish mysticism, their religious and spiritual significance and how they relate to life today.
6 x 9, 224 pp, Quality PB, 978-1-58023-200-5 **$18.99**; HC, 978-1-58023-029-2 **$21.95**

The Way Into Jewish Prayer
By Lawrence A. Hoffman
Opens the door to 3,000 years of Jewish prayer, making available all anyone needs to feel at home in the Jewish way of communicating with God.
6 x 9, 208 pp, Quality PB, 978-1-58023-201-2 **$18.99**

The Way Into Judaism and the Environment
By Jeremy Benstein
Explores the ways in which Judaism contributes to contemporary social-environmental issues, the extent to which Judaism is part of the problem and how it can be part of the solution.
6 x 9, 288 pp, HC, 978-1-58023-268-5 **$24.99**

The Way Into *Tikkun Olam* (Repairing the World)
By Elliot N. Dorff
An accessible introduction to the Jewish concept of the individual's responsibility to care for others and repair the world.
6 x 9, 320 pp, HC, 978-1-58023-269-2 **$24.99**

The Way Into Torah
By Norman J. Cohen
Helps guide in the exploration of the origins and development of Torah, explains why it should be studied and how to do it.
6 x 9, 176 pp, Quality PB, 978-1-58023-198-5 **$16.99**; HC, 978-1-58023-028-5 **$21.95**

The Way Into the Varieties of Jewishness
By Sylvia Barack Fishman, PhD
Explores the religious and historical understanding of what it has meant to be Jewish from ancient times to the present controversy over "Who is a Jew?"
6 x 9, 288 pp, HC, 978-1-58023-030-8 **$24.99**

Theology/Philosophy

Christians and Jews in Dialogue: Learning in the Presence of the Other
By Mary C. Boys and Sara S. Lee; Foreword by Dr. Dorothy Bass
6 x 9, 240 pp, HC, 978-1-59473-144-0 **$21.99** *(A SkyLight Paths book)*

The Death of Death: Resurrection and Immortality in Jewish Thought
By Neil Gillman 6 x 9, 336 pp, Quality PB, 978-1-58023-081-0 **$18.95**

Ethics of the Sages: *Pirke Avot*—Annotated & Explained
Translation & Annotation by Rabbi Rami Shapiro
5½ x 8¼, 208 pp, Quality PB, 978-1-59473-207-2 **$16.99** *(A SkyLight Paths book)*

Evolving Halakhah: A Progressive Approach to Traditional Jewish Law
By Rabbi Dr. Moshe Zemer 6 x 9, 480 pp, Quality PB, 978-1-58023-127-5 **$29.95**;
HC, 978-1-58023-002-5 **$40.00**

Hasidic Tales: Annotated & Explained
By Rabbi Rami Shapiro; Foreword by Andrew Harvey
5½ x 8¼, 240 pp, Quality PB, 978-1-893361-86-7 **$16.95** *(A SkyLight Paths Book)*

Healing the Jewish-Christian Rift: Growing Beyond our Wounded History
By Ron Miller and Laura Bernstein; Foreword by Dr. Beatrice Bruteau
6 x 9, 288 pp, Quality PB, 978-1-59473-139-6 **$18.99** *(A SkyLight Paths book)*

A Heart of Many Rooms: Celebrating the Many Voices within Judaism
By David Hartman 6 x 9, 352 pp, Quality PB, 978-1-58023-156-5 **$19.95**

The Hebrew Prophets: Selections Annotated & Explained
Translation & Annotation by Rabbi Rami Shapiro; Foreword by Zalman M. Schachter-Shalomi
5½ x 8¼, 224 pp, Quality PB, 978-1-59473-037-5 **$16.99** *(A SkyLight Paths book)*

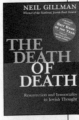

A Jewish Understanding of the New Testament
By Rabbi Samuel Sandmel; Preface by Rabbi David Sandmel
5½ x 8¼, 368 pp, Quality PB, 978-1-59473-048-1 **$19.99** *(A SkyLight Paths book)*

Keeping Faith with the Psalms: Deepen Your Relationship with God Using the Book
of Psalms *By Daniel F. Polish* 6 x 9, 320 pp, Quality PB, 978-1-58023-300-2 **$18.99**;
HC, 978-1-58023-179-4 **$24.95**

A Living Covenant: The Innovative Spirit in Traditional Judaism
By David Hartman 6 x 9, 368 pp, Quality PB, 978-1-58023-011-7 **$20.00**

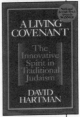

Love and Terror in the God Encounter
The Theological Legacy of Rabbi Joseph B. Soloveitchik
By David Hartman 6 x 9, 240 pp, Quality PB, 978-1-58023-176-3 **$19.95**;
HC, 978-1-58023-112-1 **$25.00**

The Personhood of God: Biblical Theology, Human Faith and the Divine Image
By Dr. Yochanan Muffs; Foreword by Dr. David Hartman
6 x 9, 240 pp, HC, 978-1-58023-265-4 **$24.99**

Tormented Master: *The Life and Spiritual Quest of Rabbi Nahman of Bratslav*
By Arthur Green 6 x 9, 416 pp, Quality PB, 978-1-879045-11-8 **$19.99**

Traces of God: Seeing God in Torah, History and Everyday Life
By Neil Gillman 6 x 9, 240 pp, HC, 978-1-58023-249-4 **$21.99**

We Jews and Jesus: Exploring Theological Differences for Mutual Understanding
By Rabbi Samuel Sandmel; Preface by Rabbi David Sandmel
6 x 9, 176 pp, Quality PB, 978-1-59473-208-9 **$16.99** *(A SkyLight Paths book)*

Your Word Is Fire: The Hasidic Masters on Contemplative Prayer
Edited and translated by Arthur Green and Barry W. Holtz
6 x 9, 160 pp, Quality PB, 978-1-879045-25-5 **$15.95**

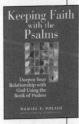

I Am Jewish
Personal Reflections Inspired by the Last Words of Daniel Pearl

Almost 150 Jews—both famous and not—from all walks of life, from all around
the world, write about Identity, Heritage, Covenant / Chosenness and Faith,
Humanity and Ethnicity, and *Tikkun Olam* and Justice.
Edited by Judea and Ruth Pearl
6 x 9, 304 pp, Deluxe PB w/flaps, 978-1-58023-259-3 **$18.99**; HC, 978-1-58023-183-1 **$24.99**
Download a free copy of the *I Am Jewish Teacher's Guide* at our website:
www.jewishlights.com

About Jewish Lights

People of all faiths and backgrounds yearn for books that attract, engage, educate, and spiritually inspire.

Our principal goal is to stimulate thought and help all people learn about who the Jewish People are, where they come from, and what the future can be made to hold. While people of our diverse Jewish heritage are the primary audience, our books speak to people in the Christian world as well and will broaden their understanding of Judaism and the roots of their own faith.

We bring to you authors who are at the forefront of spiritual thought and experience. While each has something different to say, they all say it in a voice that you can hear.

Our books are designed to welcome you and then to engage, stimulate, and inspire. We judge our success not only by whether or not our books are beautiful and commercially successful, but by whether or not they make a difference in your life.

For your information and convenience, at the back of this book we have provided a list of other Jewish Lights books you might find interesting and useful. They cover all the categories of your life:

Bar/Bat Mitzvah
Bible Study / Midrash
Children's Books
Congregation Resources
Current Events / History
Ecology
Fiction: Mystery, Science Fiction
Grief / Healing
Holidays / Holy Days
Inspiration
Kabbalah / Mysticism / Enneagram

Life Cycle
Meditation
Parenting
Prayer
Ritual / Sacred Practice
Spirituality
Theology / Philosophy
Travel
12-Step
Women's Interest

Stuart M. Matlins

Stuart M. Matlins, Publisher

Or phone, fax, mail or e-mail to: **JEWISH LIGHTS Publishing**
Sunset Farm Offices, Route 4 • P.O. Box 237 • Woodstock, Vermont 05091
Tel: (802) 457-4000 • Fax: (802) 457-4004 • www.jewishlights.com
Credit card orders: (800) 962-4544 (8:30AM–5:30PM ET Monday–Friday)
Generous discounts on quantity orders. SATISFACTION GUARANTEED. Prices subject to change.

For more information about each book, visit our website at www.jewishlights.com